PRAISE FOR NEWSFLASH!

"Teresa Tomeo's latest book, 'Newsflash! My Surprising Journey from Secular Anchor to Media Evangelist,' is one of the most riveting stories I have encountered in a very long time. I have gotten to know Teresa well over the past several years because of my weekly appearance on her radio show "Catholic Connection," and her trips to Rome where I work as EWTN's bureau chief. Reading this book is like being in Teresa's company: she writes like she talks, with conviction, passion, sincerity and dedication – and with great love for God, the Catholic Church and its teachings and her fellow man. Each page of "Newsflash" infuses the reader with that same enthusiasm, with a sense of hope, with a feeling of "I, too, can turn things around in my life." With great humility, courage and sincerity, Teresa tells us how she went from the junk food of the secular media back to the table of the Lord, to the Eucharist. We learn how Teresa allowed God back into her life and how He turned her misplaced priorities into a meaningful map for life's journey towards eternity. Everyone who reads "Newsflash" will recognize something of themselves in this book. They will see strength and weakness, pettiness and greatness, egoism and altruism. They will see that when they put their lives into God's hands, He weaves a far better tapestry than any of us can do alone. "Newsflash" will undoubtedly transform the reader. I hope it goes a step further and encourages the reader to help transform society from a secular culture that values "having" to one that values "being," from a culture that promotes "me" to one that promotes "we." One thing is certain: no reader will remain untouched or unchanged after reading "Newsflash" Every reader will give a silent "high five" to Teresa Tomeo for having shared her struggles and doubts and mistakes, her victories, her innermost thoughts and feelings, her entire heart and soul."

Joan F. Lewis
Rome Bureau Chief - EWTN

"Teresa Tomeo's latest book, 'Newsflash! My Surprising Journey from Secular Anchor to Media Evangelist,' is a humble admission of where she's been as she looks with confident assurance to the future, convinced that Our Risen Jesus—News Director and Executive Producer—is with her all the way. With compassion for those who carry the heavy cross of Christ, Teresa understands human suffering. Instead of becoming bitter from her experiences with disappointment, she became better, recognizing Our Lord's persistent call to return to the Sacraments, especially Confession and Holy Communion, and applying herself anew in following the Master. We are indebted to this gentle storyteller for allowing us this extreme close-up, which reminds us that although the camera doesn't blink, God casts away our sins in the ocean of His mercy, giving us a fresh chance to begin over."

Msgr. Charles M. Mangan
Vatican's Congregation for Institutes of Consecrated Life
and Societies of Apostolic Life
Rome, Italy

"Teresa Tomeo has shown once again the truth of the adage, 'God writes straight with crooked lines.' While I'm sure she would never have chosen the path on which the Lord has led her, I'm equally certain she wouldn't trade it for anything. As one who, like Teresa, has his professional roots in the challenging world of the secular media, and, who likewise has experienced the call of God to work in His 'electronic vineyard,' I feel keenly the power and impact of the newsflash she has so eloquently presented to her readers. It's much more than simply the story of how she rediscovered the beauty of Catholicism; it highlights how her love of the faith compels her to share it with the world."

Jerry Usher
Host of Catholic Answers Live
Co-editor of "Called By Name"
Founder and President of Third Millennium Media www.yourcatholicmedia.com

"As someone who, like Teresa, was once fooled into thinking that issues like contraception were just individual matters of choice, I appreciate the story she shares so well in her new book. I'm confident that many of our sisters-in-Christ will find in 'Newsflash!' an encouragement for their own journey."

Janet A. Morana
Associate Direction, Priests for Life
Co-Founder, Silent No More Awareness Campaign

"What a gift Teresa Tomeo is to the Church! Her voice in Catholic radio, as well as her speaking in so many places across the country, has helped many to grow in their relationship with Jesus, to better understand the teachings of the Church, and to discover practical ways they can become active in the media to transform the culture of death into a culture of life. In sharing her personal story with us, she provides an intimate look into how the Lord has been at work in her life through the good times and the bad. I think everyone will be able to relate to her wit, candor and honesty and, hopefully, as a result, see how the same Lord may be working in their lives as well."

Father John Riccardo
Ave Maria Radio
Pastor Our Lady of Good Counsel Parish, Plymouth, MI

"In this brilliant and compelling read, the sensuous comforts of our American lives come crashing head-to-head with the life-changing truths which come only through Christ Himself. Teresa's candor woos us into her very private story and allows each man to see himself in her behaviors. Her work is clearly inspired by God Himself."

'Newsflash' should be accompanied by a warning: Do Not begin reading until you have time to finish; do not read if you are afraid of encountering Christ. Teresa's Tomeo's words are clearly inspired by God Himself."

Meg Meeker, M.D.
Author of "Boys Should be Boys: 7 Secrets to Raising Healthy Sons"

NEWSFLASH!
My Surprising Journey from Secular Anchor to Media Evangelist

Teresa Tomeo

Other books by Teresa Tomeo: *Noise: How Our Media-Saturated Culture Dominates Lives and Dismantles Families* ; available at AscensionPress.com. For information on Teresa's books, her columns and newsletter, or to ask Teresa to speak at your event, visit www.TeresaTomeo.com

"Newsflash" My Surprising Journey from Secular Anchor to Media Evangelist," along with other fine Christian fiction and non-fiction titles, is published by Bezalel Books in Waterford, MI
www.BezalelBooks.com

The following abbreviations have been used when citing important works within this book:

CC: Pius XI, *Casti Connubii* ("On Christian Marriage"); 1930
CCC: The *Catechism of the Catholic Church*
EIA: Leo XIII, *Exeunte Iam Anno* ("On the Right Ordering of Human Life"); 1888
ICUP: John Paul II, Address to the International Catholic Union of the Press; 2002
MD: John Paul II, *Mulieris Dignitatem* ("On the Dignity and Vocation of Women"); 1988
MDei: Pius XII, *Mediator Dei* ("On the Sacred Liturgy"); 1947

ISBN 978-0-9800483-9-1

Library of Congress Control Number 2008930818

This book is dedicated to:

My husband Dom, for giving me the courage to move forward. I love you.

My radio listeners who support and encourage me every day. Thank you for listening.

The gang at Ave Maria Radio: Thank you for the gift of allowing me to work with all of you in Catholic Radio. Al, you have always been an inspiration to me. To Andrew K., for all of your tireless efforts to make Catholic Connection the best it can be. To Amy, what a gift and a blessing you are to my ministry; thanks for all you do for Teresa Tomeo Communications.

My friends at EWTN; Doug K., Michelle, Joan, Johnnette, Thom, Frank, Raymond, & John. Thanks for making me part of the EWTN family.

"Ethel" ~ your friendship is such a gift ~ from "Lucy"

All of my sisters from the 2003-2007 Women's Conference. Thank you for your sisterhood and support as we continue to move forward and make a difference in His name.

Cheryl and Bezalel Books: For your dedication, patience, and creativity. Your input made all the difference in this book. Thank you!

FOREWORD

I don't remember the first time I actually saw Teresa Tomeo reporting a news event on television. She had simply been one of the lights that made up the constellation that was Detroit television news. I do, however, remember the first time she arrested my attention.

In December 1995, a fire destroyed the Society of St. Vincent de Paul's Detroit warehouse and store jeopardizing the Christmas cheer of the many families that depended on the charity. All the news outlets in Detroit reported the devastation. Teresa's reporting, however, shed the pretense of detachment that marks so much of so-called objective reporting. Securing the support of her station, she urged viewers to make a Christmas gift and restore the Society to full functioning. I hadn't seen anything quite like it in television news: a passionate professionalism. Clearly, this was a reporter who was personally invested. I remember telling my wife, Sally, "This is a sister in the Lord." And, gloriously, there was an outpouring of community support and St. Vincent de Paul bounced back with plans to rebuild.

Over the years Teresa and I became acquainted as media colleagues and then friends. In 1997, I moved to Ann Arbor at the invitation of Domino's Pizza founder, Tom Monaghan, to manage what came to be Ave Maria Radio. Teresa eventually began broadcasting at the evangelical Protestant station where I had enjoyed ten years of talk radio.

As Ave Maria Radio grew, we wanted to produce more original Catholic programming. I thought of Teresa immediately. Her Catholic faith had become increasingly clear and focused and she was beginning to kick against the goals of the Protestant station's format. (There is great humor in all of this. The station's program director, a friend and former colleague, was charged by station management with reining in her Catholicism. But he was himself preparing to enter the Catholic Church and eventually left to host his own Catholic program.) In the Providence of God, Teresa was able to begin Catholic Connection produced by Ave Maria Radio in December of 2002.

I say, in the Providence of God, with some real justification. Just two months later, in February of 2003, I was hospitalized with necrotizing fasciitis, the 'flesh-eating' bacteria. For nearly a week doctors labored to keep me on earth. The Ave Maria staff was exceptionally dedicated but also exceptionally young and, at that time, relatively inexperienced. Besides myself, Teresa was the only veteran member of our on-air team. That terrible night, our mutual friend, Steve Ray, drove home the point in a phone conversation with her: "If Al doesn't make it through this crisis, the burden is going to fall on you." Teresa tells me she was frantic. "I can't do it. It will be too much." Steve reassured her that God had prepared for such a time as this. He had.

I wouldn't return to host "Kresta in the Afternoon" for six months. For a number of those months Teresa not only did her program but, along with Nick Thomm, filled in for me and consulted with our general manager, Mike Jones, as he kept a hand on the rudder. Her presence went a long way to reassure listeners and staff that Ave Maria Radio was continuing. To this day, she continues to play a vital role in this radio apostolate. Which brings me to why I am writing the Foreword to her testimony book: Simply, I am one of those blessed by her media work.

Many of Teresa's friends and fans have been after her to put her story in book form. We've often only picked it up in dribs and drabs. At last we have a coherent story and it's been worth the wait.

Hers is a tale for our times. It moves briskly, sped along by her distinct voice and personality. You will feel the amphetamine of media competition as it euthanizes her Catholic girlhood. When her career takes off, expectations grow extravagant, compromises creep in, rewarding relationships grow feeble. She turns her back on her God and neglects the love of her husband. The media seduction complete, the glamorous world of journalism itself grows fickle. But she undergoes mysterious changes even 'as the news-world turns.' Christ slips back into her life to destroy the work of the devil. Years of misplaced love and loyalty are restored. Bad news gives way to the Good News and a new apostolate is born.

Teresa's story has, and will continue to shout, hope to many women entangled by the contradictory and impossible promises of the world. She is as instructive as she is colorful. Her portrayal of ongoing conversion is pointed and realistic and she doesn't mislead by glittering promises of 'just believe and everything will be fixed.' Throughout "NewsFlash," God is off-camera, ready and able to break through at any moment. When He does we get a taste of the glory, the greatness of Woman, a truth that mere celebrity can never seriously offer. I am humbled by the small role I've played in such a wonderful story of redemptive love.

Al Kresta
President and CEO, Ave Maria Radio
Host of "Kresta in the Afternoon"

There is no power so great
in all the world
as a woman
when she falls in love
with Jesus Christ

Father John Hardon, S.J.
July 22, 1988

TABLE OF CONTENTS

INTRODUCTION

News happens! That's a slogan emblazoned on a favorite t-shirt of mine. You're probably more familiar with the phrase "life happens." But I am a news person with now more than 27 years in radio, TV, and print journalism under my belt so I tend to look at the world through, shall we say, newsprint colored glasses? News reporting is like breathing to me. I have that nose for news that can sniff out the story and turn it around on the air, or in print, under the most demanding of deadlines. I believe there is always a story to be told somewhere by someone.

Worthy are you, Lord our God, to receive glory and honor and power, for you created all things; because of your will they came to be and were created.

Revelation 4:11

All of us have a beautiful, developing story to share; a story that continues to be written by the author of life, the Lord God Himself. That's why while formulating the outline for this book, I realized that much of the terminology used to describe various aspects of the news or journalism profession is also applicable to the ups and downs of our every day lives. Those sudden and unexpected problems, or changes, that occur are very much like *"newsflashes"* or *"bulletins"* from God that grab our attention and test our strength and our faith.

Each of our lives encompass the *"Five W's and the H: The who, what, where, when, why, and how."* Those basic key questions or elements that help us prioritize and then re-prioritize along the way. As painful as it may sometimes be, we all need to zoom in to the *"extreme close-up"* of our lives and take a good long look through the spiritual lens of our faith to see if we are doing our best to live a Godly life. Do we really believe that God is in charge or is someone else sitting in the director's chair, calling the shots and pushing the buttons in our personal *"Master Control"* room? I think you can see why it is especially fitting to apply some of the more common news language to describe the big breaking news story of life, especially the life of a media person.

My particular journey has often seemed like a very surprising one as it moved from that of a secular anchor to media evangelist. And yet, in retrospect, it has all made sense. Just as your life, too, makes sense when guided by God. After all, there are no surprises to our all-knowing and all-loving Father. Only to us!

It is my privilege to share with you my own surprises, my husband's surprises, and even the surprises of my broadcasting colleagues and close friends. And in the sharing reveal how life, yours and mine, is truly an anointed, "developing story." If we are still on this earth it is because the good Lord isn't through with any of us yet! This is exciting news worth proclaiming.

If you have found yourself exhausted or discouraged from your journey, I am here to be your personal cheerleader – don't give up. You have been saved by Christ and your journey is intended to help you grow in your relationship with Him. So, stay tuned…

And may I ask that you pray for me that I will continue to be open to the signals God sends me. I pray you find my story helpful in your own walk with Jesus. My prayers are with you, as well, in the knowledge that our journeys are meant to give glory to His kingdom, now and in the age to come.

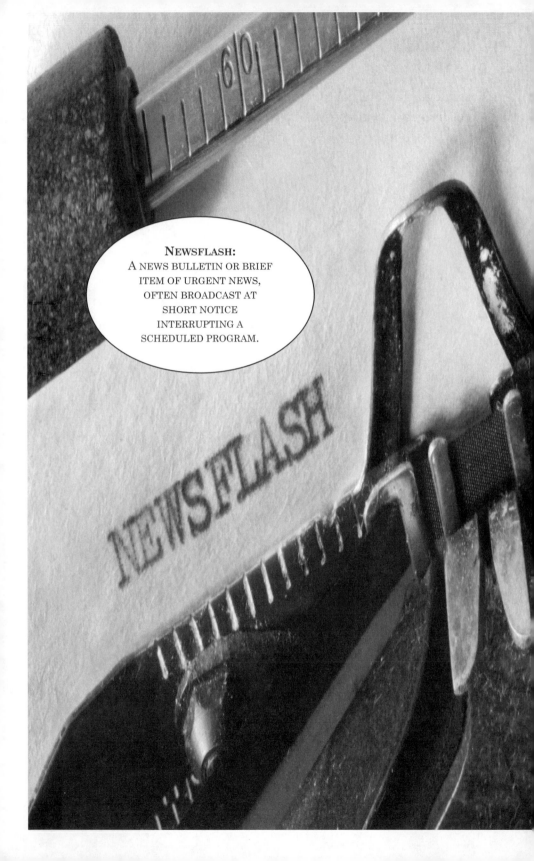

NEWSFLASH:
A NEWS BULLETIN OR BRIEF
ITEM OF URGENT NEWS,
OFTEN BROADCAST AT
SHORT NOTICE
INTERRUPTING A
SCHEDULED PROGRAM.

CHAPTER ONE
"Newsflash"

We've all heard and seen them countless times, especially during those infamous TV and radio ratings periods. You know the dramatic "newsflash" or "bulletin" that comes thundering onto the screen and over the air waves with the strong music bed underneath the booming voice of the announcer.

The bulletins interrupt our favorite program to tell us about the big news breaking locally, nationally, or maybe even internationally. *We interrupt this broadcast* or *this just into our newsroom* are two of the familiar phrases we hear. Regardless of the subject matter, the style or delivery of the newsflash itself is always alarming, jarring, and quite unsettling. In other words it is designed to make you sit up and take notice...and it works!

From this point of view, the "woman" is the representative and the archetype of the whole human race: she represents the humanity which belongs to all human beings, both men and women.

John Paul II, MD

Ironically, or maybe appropriately, it was a news bulletin much like the ones I just described that helped confirm the need for formulating my testimony into a book. It was this same newsflash concerning an old acquaintance of mine that brought me to my knees and made me even more grateful for the grace and mercy of God.

It was a Saturday afternoon in late February of 2008. Two weeks earlier I had attended a powerful congress in Rome focusing on the 20th anniversary of John Paul II's beautiful letter *Mulieris Dignitatem* ("On the Dignity and Vocation of Women"). I was chosen as one of only 250 delegates from around the world to attend the gathering and to this day it was one of the most powerful faith-based conferences I have ever experienced. The Rome gathering, "Woman-Man/Humanum in Its Entirety" featured a variety of different presenters including Bible scholars, theologians, law professors, Cardinals, and international pro-life activists. The world congress was convened by the Pontifical Council for the Laity for a specific purpose:

> *To review the progress of women over the past twenty years, to open up a reflection regarding new cultural paradigms, to collaborate with men in building up the Church and society, and to remind women of the beauty of the vocation to holiness.*

It was a chance for the delegates to go deep into the Church's teachings concerning women, especially the teachings of our late Holy Father, John Paul II.

As I was driving around town running my usual errands to the cleaners and the supermarket, I continued to ask God to help me share what I learned in Rome with my listeners. I was thinking about all the female friends and relatives in my life who could benefit from the information, especially those who had fallen away from the faith. A great many women today have no idea what the Church truly teaches and have been so misled through a combination of poor catechesis and an onslaught of messages from the culture that I knew, deep within my soul, that the information from the Rome gathering needed to be disseminated.

Women are told through Hollywood, media bias, advertising, and the ideology of radical feminism that they should sacrifice everything for the sake of their own desires and needs. They are told Christianity, especially Catholicism, is an oppressive "no," when it is really, as Pope Benedict XVI says, "a big yes." In our private audience with the Holy Father during the Rome congress, he stressed the fallout from this kind of thinking;

> *When, therefore, men or women pretend to be autonomous or totally self-sufficient, they risk being closed up in a self-realization that considers the overcoming of every natural, social or religious bond as a conquest of freedom but which in fact reduces them to an oppressive solitude.*

Countless women are still convinced that power, success, and control matter most. As a result, they join the ranks of the walking wounded. They may reach great financial and professional heights, but real happiness is nowhere to be found. So they keep searching by moving from one conquest to the next. They have no idea how precious they really are in God's eyes; precious not because of what they achieve but because they are created in His image and likeness and are daughters of the King! They are restless, as I was for so very long, because they have not yet, as St. Augustine tells us, been able to rest completely in God.

One woman in particular, whom we'll refer to as "Sandy," weighed heavily on my mind and heart that weekend. Sandy was a former colleague. We worked side by side as television news reporters for several years. Our similar backgrounds soon brought us together as friends. We were both raised Catholic. We were both Italian American and we were both driven by similar career goals.

We were hungry to make a name for ourselves in the competitive Metropolitan Detroit television news market.

Sandy was a smart, beautiful, and a talented journalist who at one point had it all, at least according to our personal standards at the time and most certainly according to the world's standards. I admired her and enjoyed being in her company. She was a few years younger than I was but had already achieved the upscale lifestyle I so desired. She lived in a stunning home, wore designer clothes, and also managed to buck the feminist trend by getting married to a handsome man and raising beautiful children. As they say, "She had it all."

At some point, however, her world started to change. Sadly, it began with her marriage which became rocky and with life quickly becoming difficult, the personal problems eventually became such that they forced her to leave the news business. Divorce followed, and then a series of very troubling public events occurred. This news reporter who once delivered the headlines was now making headlines herself.

Sandy was arrested for shoplifting and was later ticketed for drunken driving. Soon thereafter the child custody battles began followed, a year or so later, by charges of embezzlement.

The embezzlement story broke earlier in the week and that Saturday afternoon, not long after attending the Rome gathering, I listened to reports about the charges against Sandy as the terrible news filled the airwaves and stopped me in my tracks. My car radio was tuned, as it normally is, to the all-news station but I was unprepared for what I was about to hear.

This just into our newsroom, a former local TV reporter has been found dead in her suburban Detroit home. The

> *immediate cause of death is unknown but sources close to the scene say the former Detroit news woman may have committed suicide.*

I felt like someone had kicked me in the stomach. I started banging on the steering wheel and screaming "No!" I couldn't imagine that Sandy would take matters this far or that she could ever be that desperate. Within a matter of hours the cause of death was confirmed as suicide. I shared the sad news with my husband Dominic and then some powerful flashbacks started to occur for both of us. We recalled all the lavish parties in Sandy's fabulous home and even admitted some of the jealousies we had experienced.

Dominic and I were beginning to struggle in our marriage, at the time, and to us Sandy was living the American dream. She was so bubbly and energetic, and she was able to take care of the kids, entertain a houseful, and then put in ten hours at the local station without appearing at all stressed or frazzled. Sandy and her husband seemed so happy and so perfect for each other. They were popular in high school, and seemed to take that with them into their adult lives. Who wouldn't want to be them? And who could measure up? But no one had any idea of the troubles that lurked behind the scenes.

Eventually, my husband and I returned to the Church and slowly began to heal our marriage. We became very involved in Bible studies and parish life. Sandy and I drifted apart. Although she was Catholic and sent her children to Catholic school, we were at much different points in our faith life and we no longer had much in common. I heard rumors from time to time that she was having some personal struggles but never knew the extent of her heartache. To this day I cannot get the images of this dear sister-in-Christ out of my mind. She left no note behind, and I can only imagine how she must have felt as she made the final decision to take her life. She was forty-two.

I often wonder if I am experiencing "survivor's guilt." My husband and I ask ourselves, why her? Why did her marriage end, and not ours? Why did she feel so hopeless and desperate? Could we have done something differently to help prevent such a senseless tragedy?

I may never know the answers to these questions but I do know that the particular newsflash about my former colleague provided a teachable moment, an epiphany, really. It prompted me to ponder more closely the many "newsflashes" in my own life, moments that God used to get my attention. Moments that forced me to remember that there but for the grace of Almighty God goes any one of us.

It also reminded me once again of the mercy of God; His mercy not only for me and my husband in eventually saving our relationship and guiding us back home to the Church, but also, I believe, in His mercy for Sandy. Only the Lord knows the state of someone's heart. This is another reason why I am so grateful for the teachings of the Catholic Church. The Church, in her wisdom, allows God to be God, as we read in the *Catechism:*

> *We should not despair of the eternal salvation of persons who have taken their own lives. By ways known to him alone, God can provide the opportunity for salutary repentance. The Church prays for persons who have taken their own lives. CCC #2283*

A "newsflash" is a bulletin or brief item of urgent or surprising news, often broadcast on short notice and interrupting a scheduled program. In my own life's journey God was the dramatic announcer interrupting what I thought was the perfectly written and scheduled program. I was on the same path as Sandy. I can only speak for myself but I was concentrating only on what the world convinced me was important. I was misguided, misled, and getting sucked in by the culture. Add to that the fact that I was poorly formed in my faith, which I think is the case for many of us, and you have a formula for disaster and tragedy.

Let's face it, we don't start out with bad intentions but once we get set in a certain direction and used to a particular way of living, it's hard to change. Or maybe we just don't know how to change or to whom we should turn. Most of us are simply, as that old country tune says, "looking for love [and fulfillment] in all the wrong places." I believe Sandy was a good person. For some reason, she was unable to cope with her problems and setbacks. The world told Sandy she needed to go after that brass ring but never told her what to do if or when that brass ring disappeared.

I pray that all of us may come to see how the newsflashes along the way can be wakeup calls from God. Jarring, yes. Unsettling, absolutely. Alarming - you better believe it. But if you are open to tuning out the world and tuning into God, the heavenly bulletins can lead the way to positive turning points.

And please, let us all continue to pray, with the Church, for Sandy and others who unfortunately have taken their own lives. May the Lord God have mercy on their souls.

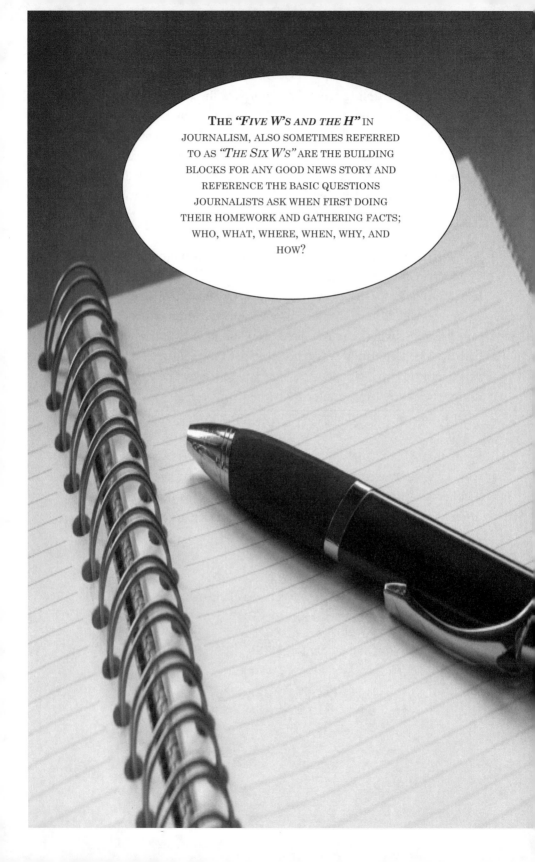

THE *"FIVE W'S AND THE H"* IN JOURNALISM, ALSO SOMETIMES REFERRED TO AS *"THE SIX W'S"* ARE THE BUILDING BLOCKS FOR ANY GOOD NEWS STORY AND REFERENCE THE BASIC QUESTIONS JOURNALISTS ASK WHEN FIRST DOING THEIR HOMEWORK AND GATHERING FACTS; WHO, WHAT, WHERE, WHEN, WHY, AND HOW?

CHAPTER TWO
"The Five W's and the H:
Who, What, Where, When, Why, and How"

*T*he Five W's and an H" is a phrase used to describe some simple, short, and to the point questions that are designed to help the journalist get to the heart of the issue or event he or she is covering. They are so applicable in my own testimony but are also applicable to your personal journey. It is my hope that in using this news jargon and sharing with you my own story you, too, will take the time to discover and embrace your own "five w's and an h."

We may ask: what does it mean to be a professional journalist who is Catholic? Quite simply, it means being a person of integrity, an individual whose personal and professional life reflects the teachings of Jesus and the Gospel.

John Paul II, ICUP

"Who" is involved in this story? I am, of course. But so are countless other people who came into my life, if only for a brief moment, and made a difference. You've already met Sandy, someone who will always have a special place in my heart, and you will meet a lot of other special people in this book as well. I will share them with you because I continue to marvel at how this amazing God we serve, in His great providence, puts all sorts of

people in our path. I want to share my knowledge with you that at very particular times, and if we are open, God uses those people to have a profound impact on us.

You, the reader, also fall under the first "who" category. If you decided to take time out of your busy schedule to read my testimony, then you are among those who might be affected by the story of my journey. If you have ever wondered where your life is going, if you have ever suffered with a troubled marriage or family relationship, if you have had a hard time forgiving yourself for the mistakes of the past, if life has thrown you some very unexpected curves and burst into your normal routine with some startling news bulletins, than you are part of this story as well. After all, there isn't one among us who hasn't been affected by "life," and it is in the sharing that we often feel comfort. Knowing that we aren't alone allows us to appreciate God's presence through others.

"What" happened in my life and prompted me to write a book about my journey from secular anchor to media evangelist? God and His Catholic Church happened. I never had any intention of working in Catholic media and sharing my personal struggles with the world. I returned to God and the faith of my youth after many years of great questioning and struggling in both my personal and professional life. I found out that God's plan is indeed the best plan, even when it's not our plan. Go figure! And I have found in sharing my story with my radio listeners, and at conferences and seminars around the country, that "what" happened to me has happened to so many other people, especially those of us who are Baby Boomers.

[What does it mean to be a professional journalist who is Catholic?] It means offering examples of hope and heroism to a world that is in desperate need of both.

John Paul II, ICUP

We left behind the faith of our youth to search somewhere far over the rainbow for something we thought would be much better, something the culture and the world told us was worth pursuing. We found out, after many trials and tribulations, that we had everything we needed right in front of us. We never really had to venture further than our own backyard, as Dorothy says, to discover true happiness and fulfillment. It was there all along in Christ and His one, holy, Catholic, and apostolic Church.

But if someone would have told me fifteen or sixteen years ago that I ever would have entertained the thought of leaving the news business, I would have laughed hysterically and told them they were a few sandwiches short of a picnic. News reporting had been a part of my life for as long as I can remember. I didn't know how to do anything else, nor did I want to, or so I thought. I would have laughed even harder had they told me I would be giving lectures or writing books and columns in national newspapers concerning media influence and activism. Never would I have imagined myself to be sharing my faith testimony and hosting a Catholic radio show, of all crazy things.

Remember, I idolized the news media and thought we could do no wrong. I was proud to be part of the media culture, and felt we were doing great things. My Catholic faith had become a distant memory, something that was hauled out and brushed off twice a year for major holidays, or was a quick fix when I needed an answer to a troubling situation. On occasion it was the "in" or "ticket" I needed when I was sent to cover a story involving a local archdiocese. I considered myself a Christian, but in reality I had little understanding of Scripture, and even less understanding of the Catholic Church's rich heritage and teachings. I had a grasp of the basics, but beyond that my world was secular.

"Where" does my story unfold? The geographical location of my particular story centers on my home state of Michigan and my hometown of suburban Detroit. This is where I was raised in the faith, attended journalism school, met and married my wonderful husband Dominic, and began my professional communications career in 1981. Metropolitan Detroit is where I still live and work today. Although my radio show is syndicated nationally, the show is produced by Ave Maria Radio in southeastern Michigan and distributed through EWTN Global Catholic Radio. I will be sharing some interesting tales of events I've covered that occurred in and around the Motor City. I will also try to explain how my experience in the Detroit news media, some good and some bad, eventually impacted my decision to leave the secular media to pursue work in Christian communications and public speaking.

Detroit, however, is really just the backdrop for my story. We need to really "zoom in" as we say in the TV news business, on the central location or the real "where" in my story, and that would be the Roman Catholic Church. It is this Church into which I was received as an infant through the Sacrament of Baptism. Through the Catholic Church I met and fell in love with Jesus. But like so many young people growing up in the 60's and 70's, I was fickle and soon fled the scene, so to speak, for what I thought would be more exciting and satisfying relationships or partners: success, money, and fame. And, as we also say in broadcasting "stay tuned" for further details about that breaking story! But, as you have most certainly imagined, I eventually found my way back to the Catholic Church, giving firm credibility to the old saying: Home is indeed "where" the heart is.

"When" did my story begin? It began for me, as it begins for all of us, at baptism. But the story continues to this day. We all are, or should still be, on the path of discovery. After all, we are all pilgrims, sojourners, or travelers. This life on planet Earth is not our

final destination. We are meant for communion with Almighty God, a goal that won't be fully accomplished until we, Lord willing, reunite with Him in heaven. However, there have been very particular times or dates in my life that were crucial turning points that helped me get back on track. These were significant moments that I hope will help you see how God is in charge and never leaves us or forsakes us.

"Why" am I telling my story? Because in some ways I am the poster child for everything that is wrong with the culture. I admit it openly and honestly, and pray that through this public acknowledgement my story can make a difference. I bought into the lies and, as you will read, suffered greatly for my actions. Sadly, I came close to losing my precious God-given marriage, but also my soul. Thankfully, we serve a God of second, third, fourth, and countless chances. God pulled me out of the pit and gave me a new heart and a new life, one so much more meaningful than I could have ever imagined. So to whom much is given, much is expected. I would have a lot of explaining to do if I didn't share my story.

> *It means having the courage to seek and report the truth, even when the truth is inconvenient or is not considered "politically correct."*
>
> John Paul II, ICUP

The Christian life is not for wimps, especially for the Christian worshipping in the Catholic Church. If you don't want to learn about spiritual pruning and redemptive suffering, then you might want to put this book back on the shelf. On the other hand, if you are ready to learn about how all things, even the ugliest of sins and problems in your life, can work together for good, well then, read on.

Jesus tells us that we must take up our cross and follow Him. If we want to save our life, we must first lose it for His sake. John Paul II said we must become a "gift of self" and that we "won't find ourselves until we lose ourselves in Christ." I've learned just how true and redeeming these words are, and I feel a great sense of responsibility toward Sandy, and other souls like her who may be struggling to find themselves and, more importantly, to find God. It might even be worth suggesting that it is in finding God that we find our true selves.

"How" did I journey from the life of an aggressive, self-centered secular anchor to a media evangelist? Only by the grace and love of Almighty God does anything happen to any of us. The grace is there for every human being. Faith comes by first hearing the word of God, as St. Paul tells us in Romans 10:17, and then from our affirmative response, our "yes." But the grace of God, or the "how" part, still leaves me speechless and gives me chills. There are many times, maybe when I am about to give a presentation or go on the air, that I stop and ask "Lord *how* did I get here?"

Sure, I know I responded and eventually said "yes" but really, when you see the terrible mess I made of things before God came back into my life, the "how" is even more miraculous. But all of our lives are individual miracles and help us enter more deeply into the mystery of God. Indeed, by His grand design they are meant to bring us into a deeper relationship with Him.

I hope as I attempt to outline more fully the *"Five W's and the H"* in my walk with God, that the answers help you in some way. Yes, life can be difficult. If we are Christian we know that. Jesus tells us in John 16:32 that "in this world we will have trouble." But He also tells us to take heart for "He has overcome the world." Whatever your pain, whatever your heartache, Jesus and the fullness of the faith found in the Catholic Church is the answer. Don't despair.

When you read my story you will see how even after the darkest of nights, the dawn still comes. Yes, life is what happens to us while we are making plans. But don't let the troubles get you side-tracked. We will, no doubt, continue to hit bumps in the road. But life is an amazing gift. Don't be afraid to hand the remote control over to God, so He can fine-tune the prime time program of your own life. And remember, the joy is still in the journey, especially when you put the Lord in the driver's seat. So, "rise and let us be on our way" (John 14:32).

EXTREME CLOSE-UP:
A PHOTOGRAPHIC TERM
USED TO DESCRIBE A TYPE
OF CAMERA FRAMING OF A
SCENE OR PERSON THAT
PROVIDES A CLOSER VIEW
THAN A CONVENTIONAL
CLOSE-UP

CHAPTER THREE
"Extreme Close-Up"

I was surrounded by people who were enamored by the fact that they were standing near a local TV personality. Normally this kind of attention would give my already inflated ego an even bigger boost, but on this particular day I never felt more alone or more humiliated.

"Hey, I just watched you on the news the other night," one man blurted out loudly.

"I know you. You're that news lady, Teresa Tomeo," another man said, chiming in on the already uncomfortable situation that was developing as I stood in the long line at the unemployment office.

> *To become a child in relation to God is the condition for entering the kingdom. For this, we must humble ourselves and become little.*
>
> CCC #526

I wanted to snap back, "No I am not Teresa Tomeo. I just look like her. People tell me that all the time." But I knew it was too late. The gig was up, and I was already recognized. Now I would have to explain why I was filing for unemployment and joining the ranks of many of Michigan's other jobless citizens instead of covering Michigan's economic problems, as I had done so often in my years as a broadcast-journalist in Metropolitan Detroit. Pitiful clichés filled my head and my heart sunk with the realization that the shoe was, indeed, on the other foot.

Normally I was the one who would use the reporter's notepad and the lens of the TV camera as the finely sharpened tools that helped me zoom in tightly on that *"extreme close-up"* of the suffering subject. Suddenly the tables, along with the cameras, had turned dramatically, and the reporter was the center of the story. I was stunned, in a state of semi-shock after being abruptly fired just a few days earlier. One minute I was covering the lead story on the 10PM news, and the next morning, after a quick meeting with the news director and station business manager, I was walking out the door with my box of personal belongings in hand. It was difficult to comprehend that this was what my career had come down to: a cardboard box filled with a few meaningless items.

As far as I could see, which really wasn't very far as my vision at the time was quite myopic, my future looked pretty grim. The fallout from the type of life I had been living was slowly being revealed to me. Fortunately, in God's great mercy, He held my hand and revealed to me, a piece at a time, how my life had gotten off track. I began to see that I had spent so much time and energy trying to make a name for myself in the Detroit news market that I had terribly neglected my marriage, my immediate family, and close friends. My relationships with the people I cared most about were in a shambles, and since my entire identity was in my career, or "Teresa Tomeo the Newscaster," outside of the newsroom my identity was a mystery to me. At the time it seemed to be the worst thing that I could have experienced.

Eventually, however, it would turn out to be the absolute biggest blessing of my life. As Scripture tells us so beautifully in Romans 8:28: *All things work together for good for those who love the Lord and are called according to his purpose.* Still, it would take a lot of pruning on God's part, and struggling on my end, to move forward and embrace both that scripture verse as well as God's plan for my life. And it has been my experience since then, having heard the stories of so many others, that this is a truth for all of us. We serve a great and loving God who will spend the time pruning, even as we struggle, because He truly wants the very best for us.

In the modern period, from the beginning of the industrial age, the Christian truth about work had to oppose the various trends of materialistic and economistic thought.

John Paul II, LE

If you're in the broadcasting business the question is not *if* you're going to get fired, downsized, or laid off, but *when*. Broadcasting is, by its very nature, a brutal profession. Just consider some of the stories that circulate regarding news celebrities and the amounts of monies negotiated for contracts of anchors and you begin to see why the business is so cut-throat.

As far as the on-air personality goes, one day management will proclaim that you're the greatest thing since sliced bread, and the next day you are, quite frankly, old news. My firing should not have come as such a shock given that I had over ten years experience at the time. In college I had been taught by some of the great college journalism professors, people who had worked in the industry and were very open and honest about the challenges of a media career. In addition, I had already had the experience of a lay-off from a previous media position in radio. Although, admittedly, that lay-off was much easier to take than the firing.

Back in the 80's when I was starting out, radio offered a bit more anonymity. Stations didn't have web sites or web cams. There might be a 8x10 glossy of you here and there, but unless you were seen at public functions it was easy to move in and out of daily life pretty much unnoticed. And while I spoke at an occasional function after I was off the air, my career was just starting and I wasn't "in the public eye" as they say. This anonymity enabled me to bounce back emotionally from the lay-off fairly quickly. It was also easier to find a job because there are, and always have been, more radio stations in most cities than TV stations, and therefore more positions. So the overall potential for humiliation was kept at bay.

Television news, however, is much different! A television news reporting position, or anchoring job, is a much more coveted position because it usually means more money and more status. It is a prize worth obtaining because it says, "I am this good!" Your face is beamed into viewer's homes several times a day, five days a week. You are considered a celebrity. People recognize you at the mall or the grocery story and yes, as I learned, even at the unemployment office! They feel they know you and tend to ask very personal questions. For quite a while I was often asked why I was no longer on the local TV news.

Frankly, I didn't have an answer because I was never really given one. I was just told that the station was "going in a different direction." Unfortunately that's an all too common company line, and it leaves you with so many unknowns. What did I do wrong? Could I have worked harder or done something differently to secure my position? What was it about my performance that was no longer seen as productive or appealing? Wasn't it clear that I was willing to change directions? We all struggle with these sorts of questions when life throws us punches. Our first reaction is to convince ourselves and our God that we don't deserve whatever circumstances we find ourselves in but with His grace, and our effort, we find an ability to begin to move past those first haunting questions and into a frame of mind and heart where we move forward with our trust placed firmly in God.

But at the time I simply had no answers, only dozens of other questions on my mind. And, from what it looked like, lots of questions were also on the minds of the viewers staring at me as I moved along the unemployment line. What was I doing here? Why was I putting myself through this?

My husband even suggested I delay filing for benefits or forgo it altogether. We were financially stable and he was concerned that the process would be more salt in a very raw emotional wound. He was right, but as usual I didn't listen. I told him it was no big deal. I could handle it, and I might as well receive some income while I was looking for another job. So there I was in the unemployment line. Talk about the exalted being humbled! The one who grilled politicians and corporate executives on a regular basis was nervous about being interviewed and filing a few papers.

People like a juicy story, and my public termination was great copy. I dreaded facing the government worker behind the glass window who would review my paperwork and determine whether I qualified for benefits. What kind of questions would she ask? I didn't pray much back then, but on this fateful day in late October of 1993, I was certainly mustering up as many Hail Mary's as humanly possible, praying that the clerk, at least, would not recognize me and quickly move on to the next person so I could get out of that office and head home.

I wouldn't have believed it if you told me back then, but the Lord would eventually show me how to use this uncomfortable experience to help others. At that point in my life, though, it was still all about me. For a few weeks after my firing I tried to keep myself busy organizing audition tapes for interviews, updating my resume, and calling my media friends to see if there were any openings at other TV news departments around town. Despite all the contacts and friends I had made, very few people returned my phone calls. I had a great reputation for being a "team player" and never turning down an assignment. So I was starting to get worried about the lack of response to my job inquiries. I also found out that I didn't have as many friends as I thought. Suddenly it was as if I had the plague, or that my firing was contagious.

I was always very popular, and invited to all the right parties including major charity events and social gatherings involving the local media. I went from long days in the field reporting the news to long nights of socializing at the bars or at the homes of fellow reporters and news anchors. I lost count of how many weekends, holidays, and evenings I sacrificed. I kept telling myself, my husband, and my parents that I would be there for this anniversary party or that birthday celebration, but then the assignment editor would call and ask if I could fill in or cover a breaking story, or the news gang would be meeting at the local pub near the station, and I was off to the races again.

I was convinced the sacrifices would pay off, that I would be rewarded with a promotion or pay raise. After all, I was considered, for a time, the "it" girl in the local news. One of the daily newspapers did a major photo spread and story on my work. I had accumulated a shelf full of news awards and citations and was even named "Outstanding Female on Air" by the Detroit Chapter of the American Women in Radio and TV. I was making it, I told myself and my husband. Not realizing that what I was actually "making" was a big fat mess of my life.

This world has really sold us a bill of goods, hasn't it? This materialistic society that we live in tells us that we should struggle and sacrifice to get the education, the career, the big house, the sports car, and all the other *"things."* Let me tell you that my husband and I had accumulated a lot of *"things,"* alright. Before I was fired from my first TV position, we had moved into a new home, were both making a very nice living, and had achieved a decent amount of professional success. My husband was quickly moving up the corporate ladder at his architectural engineering firm. We dressed well, dined at all the nice restaurants, and vacationed along what's known as Michigan's Gold Coast, in the lovely lakeside communities of Petoskey and Charlevoix. We were close to becoming carbon copies of "Sandy" and her husband. That's what we both thought it took to be truly happy.

Dominic was the first to notice something was rotten in Denmark. Despite our success, he felt empty and started to search for answers. He shared some of his feelings with me, but I brushed them off as a phase he was going through. How could he not be happy I thought? I had a taste of the good life and wanted more… and more.

The disordered desire for money cannot but produce perverse effects.

CCC #2424

Now the phone that used to ring off the hook, bringing countless invitations, did not ring at all. The awards sat there on the family room shelves collecting dust, more reminders of my bleak situation. All the time and effort I put into my career seemed to amount to nothing, literally. It was a rude awakening, but one that I apparently needed even though I wasn't quite yet willing to embrace it.

I was growing angrier by the minute. I simply could not fathom that the world was ignoring me, an award winning, invitation-getting, headline reporting "it" girl. Of course that was a fairly arrogant thought, given the fact that I put little effort into close relationships and especially my relationship with God. I had long since stopped going to Mass, and only prayed, in urgent situations, such as the embarrassing time on the unemployment line.

My husband, although very supportive, was distant and didn't know quite how to connect with me or help me. Who could blame him? I had put my job in front of my marriage so often that I knew he was simply trying to protect himself from getting hurt or disappointed again. I had never taken much time to learn how he felt, especially when his feelings didn't match my own feelings or desires.

We are told in Galatians 6:6-10 that we reap what we sow.

> *Do not be deceived. God will not be mocked. A man reaps what he sows. The one who sows to please his sinful nature, from that nature will reap destruction; the one who sows to please the Spirit, from the Spirit will reap eternal life.*

I had sowed my sinful nature, putting only my ambitions and needs first and now I could feel the camera moving in for the extreme close-up; the tight shot that zooms in slowly to expose intimate emotions and details. Although I did my best to block the camera shot, eventually I had nothing but time on my hands, and was forced to look deeply in the camera lens. I felt like the focus of a "60 Minutes" investigation. I was now in the hot seat, sweating and squirming and very afraid of what might be revealed. Maybe even at some level, I had known what was to be revealed but did not want to face that truth. Eventually I was able to begin the painful process of self examination or, as the Catholic Church teaches, make an examination of conscience. The *Catechism* states the need for this necessary practice.

> *It is important for every person to be sufficiently present to himself in order to hear and follow the voice of his conscience. This requirement of interiority is all the more necessary as life often distracts us from any reflection, self-examination or introspection. CCC #1779*

Indeed, my career and ambitions had distracted me and now God was providing me with an opportunity for interiority and I didn't like what I was seeing. Who was this woman who had forgotten or abandoned the faith of her childhood? How did I think that my marriage would not be impacted by endless nights at the office? Why was I so willing to put so much energy into my job but so little into my marriage and my relationship with God? What was I thinking? These were some heavy questions that would take months, even years to answer.

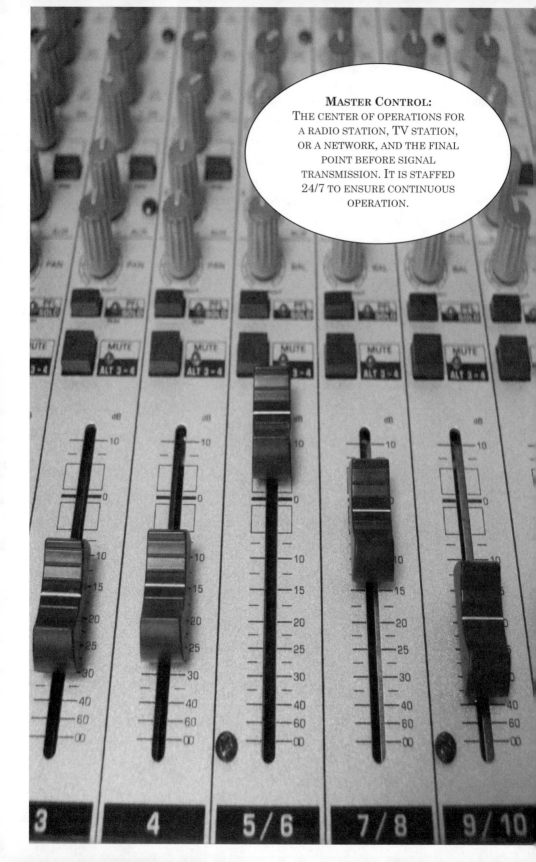

MASTER CONTROL:
THE CENTER OF OPERATIONS FOR A RADIO STATION, TV STATION, OR A NETWORK, AND THE FINAL POINT BEFORE SIGNAL TRANSMISSION. IT IS STAFFED 24/7 TO ENSURE CONTINUOUS OPERATION.

CHAPTER FOUR
"Master Control"

There's an old saying that most of us who have struggled in our faith can appreciate: *If you are not as close to God as you used to be, it is because you moved.* Since we know from Hebrews 13:8 that *Jesus is the same yesterday and today and forever,* we also know deep down, even if we don't want to admit it, that the problem is with us and not with the Lord.

I moved away from God – slowly, almost imperceptibly, so that I didn't quite recognize what was happening. Little by little I stopped practicing my Catholic faith and became what my pastor calls a "C & E" (Christmas and Easter) Christian. Everything in my life seemed to be going, for the most part, exceptionally well; thank you very much. I didn't think I needed God. I was getting along fine on my own. I felt as if I were the one making sure the right things were happening in my life and I was easily able to take credit. I graduated from journalism school and quickly made a name for myself in the news business. I met and married a great guy. Life was good. Actually, life was very good!

> *For in truth, most men, with little care whence they come or whither they go, place all their thoughts and care upon the weak and fleeting goods of this life.*
>
> Pope Leo XIII, EIA

So much so that when the rug was pulled out from under me, I came to the painful realization that I didn't know how to handle disappointment and discouragement. Neither had really been on my radar, to any real degree, and their appearance led, for a time being, to despair. Ironically, I had become weak in my belief that I was strong and in charge. I now needed to understand that my weakness was based on my own day-to-day decisions and choices. Bit by bit I had allowed some very negative influences to sit in the director's chair of my personal Master Control room, to push all the buttons and call all the wrong shots. I had replaced God with the secular messages that I have since come to rally against. The end result, while not exactly a pretty picture, has now made me driven to share with others the fallacies of what our world teaches. Like so many people who experience difficult and trying times, I can't say that I would have asked for the experience and yet can now embrace it as bringing me back to God and putting Him in charge.

How did the image on my screen get so blurry and full of static? Pope Benedict says *put simply, we are no longer able to hear God; there are too many frequencies filling our ears.* As I wrote in my first book, *Noise: How Our Media Saturated Culture Dominates Lives and Dismantles Families,* much of the noise in our lives comes from the culture, primarily the mass media. If we don't allow God to be in control, and at the center of our lives, then we can easily be influenced or manipulated by the messages we receive. That's exactly what happened to me.

I attended eight years of Catholic school in suburban Detroit, and my elementary school was run by the wonderful Sisters of St. Joseph. The sisters did a great job of teaching the faith and when I made my first Holy Communion, something clicked. In third grade it obviously wasn't head knowledge but the knowledge of the heart that allowed me to see Jesus in the Eucharist. I loved Him and I knew He was real.

From that point on, I felt God's presence instinctively when I walked into a Catholic Church. For a communion present my parents bought me a beautiful statue of the child Jesus. He was holding a chalice and at the base of the statue on either side of Jesus were two angels and underneath the words *Panis Angelicus* ("Bread of Angels"). My mother suggested I keep it under my pillow as a reminder that Jesus was always close to me.

Forty-some years later, Jesus is still under my pillow, none the worse for wear. I see that as a little miracle in itself; God reminding me that He would never leave me or forsake me. I may have forgotten about the Lord but He had never forgotten about me. He remained close to me always. It is no small miracle that I never lost that statue, even though I went from home to college. At college I moved from one dormitory to the next and then several moves after college graduation and marriage. That statue is a constant reminder that God remains by my side.

Along with dispensing valuable catechetical knowledge, the Sisters of St. Joseph were also wonderful at helping the students identify and use their talents. My gift for gab was recognized at an early age, and I was often called upon to read out loud. It was my third grade homeroom teacher, Sr. Lucinda, who asked me to take part in the school's Christmas pageant. The event is another one of those "newsflashes" or turning points in my life. My part in the production was small. I was given a few lines to read from a Christmas poem. But it meant my first shot at stardom. I would be on stage in the gym with all of my classmates watching.

> *Christmas is a tree with lights all aglow.*
> *Christmas is a candy cane with fresh and glistening snow.*

I read my lines flawlessly . . . and I was hooked. I remember it was excitement, not nervousness, I felt when the curtains were drawn and I was standing on stage staring out at the entire student body. I heard my voice travel from the microphone over the loud speakers into the gym, and it was thrilling. I was only seven, maybe eight years old at the time, but even then I knew that my voice would one day reach a much larger audience. I couldn't fathom exactly what that meant, but I could see a lot of microphones in my future!

My English teachers noticed that I was able to read quickly, maintain a high level of retention, and that I was also a strong writer. Those gifts, combined with the gift of gab, seemed to mesh perfectly for a future career in broadcast journalism. And that became my goal. I graduated from elementary school in 1973. Women were just starting to gain some ground in TV and radio news, and I idolized Barbara Walters and Liz Trotta. Walters (who is at the bottom of my favorite journalists list now for a number of reasons) at the time was making headlines herself as she struggled her way to the top of a male dominated industry. Liz Trotta, now a Fox News contributor, was the first woman to cover the war for a broadcast network. The early 70's, of course, are also associated with Watergate and Woodward and Bernstein. This added to my interest and desire to pursue journalism.

Despite my Catholic upbringing, I was unable to resist the pull of the world. My parents did their very best to instill in us a love for the Catholic faith. We never missed Mass together as a family. However, in those days most parents, mine included, left much of the faith formation up to the Catholic school system. It's just the way it was done. They hoped that sending their children to a good Catholic school, along with providing the examples at home, would be enough to keep their children in the Church. In fact many parents made significant financial sacrifices to send their children to parochial school. Unfortunately, as good as my early catechesis was, that formation took a drastic decline after I received the Sacrament of Confirmation. This was around my eighth grade year.

As a result, following graduation from Catholic grade school, my faith life was for the most part limited to weekly Mass observance. We had the constant reminders of the Church and God in our home; the crucifix, the statues of the Blessed Mother and the Infant of Prague, and of course my Jesus statue stuck securely under my pillow. These images, though, could not compete with the secular desires that were taking hold of me, including the desire to be thin, which led to the challenges of an eating disorder.

With docile hearts, then, let all Christians hearken to the voice of their Common Father, who would have them, each and every one, intimately united with him as they approach the altar of God, professing the same faith, obedient to the same law, sharing in the same Sacrifice with a single intention and one sole desire.

Pope Pius XII, M.Dei

My battle with anorexia nervosa, as I will explain later, is one of the reasons I am so passionate about media awareness and activism. I was greatly affected by the many messages from the TV, magazines, and Hollywood. Keep in mind that this was back in the early 70's - before satellite TV, cable, the Internet, and all the other techno devices or "noise" we have filling our ears and our minds today, in the 21st century. I shudder every time I think of what children are exposed to in our electronic-crazy world.

I went on to complete my education at a public high school and university. In high school I worked on the newspaper, the campus radio station, and yearbook. I excelled at forensics and won several awards for public speaking. I also excelled at socializing. I rarely missed a football game or high-school dance, and during my junior year in high school I even managed to make one of the cheerleading squads.

My college years at Central Michigan University went by quickly, filled with classes during the day and jobs at the student newspaper, radio and TV stations at night and on the weekends. There was a beautiful Catholic Church across the street from my freshman dorm, which I managed to visit regularly for weekly Mass during the first semester. By the time winter term rolled around, Mass was something I did on the night before a challenging exam. I was attaining so much success on my own; I never stopped to consider that God might have something to do with it.

Every once in a while I could feel the tug of God and the Catholic Church. For example, I discovered a beautiful quote from John Paul II regarding the importance of journalists being true to their profession. The quote was in a magazine published by the Society of Professional Journalists, of which I was a student member. The pope was speaking to journalists at the United Nations as he was leaving New York after his historic visit to the U.S very early in his pontificate.

> *Be faithful to the truth and to its transmission. For truth endures; truth will not go away. Truth will not pass away or change. And I say to you, take it as my parting words to you, the service of humanity through the medium of the truth is something worthy of your best years, your finest talents, your most dedicated efforts.*

I cut that quote out of the magazine and framed it. I still have the same frame in my office today. At the time I thought it was a meaningful quote, and it made me proud to be Catholic. I thought it was great that the pope could "get" what journalism was really about, disseminating the truth and providing a great public service. But the quote wasn't enough to get me back to Church. Instead I started to see God and the Church as somewhat oppressive.

I didn't know much about Church teaching back then, but I knew enough to understand that the Church placed great importance on marriage and family. I had no interest in either, since I bought into many of the lies of the feminist movement and was determined not be bogged down by serious relationships. As a result I became a lot like the men so many feminists complained about. I am not proud to admit that this meant using men for my own pleasure or gain, and included sexual promiscuity.

You may be asking yourself by now, "How does someone who fell in love with Jesus and the Eucharist as a child, stray so far from the Church?" Well, true love must be nurtured and given attention. I was ill equipped, and did not have the tools I needed to nurture that love. I knew Jesus, but not very well; and since I wasn't receiving Him in the Eucharist regularly at that point, I drifted further and further away from Him.

Summers were not spent by the beach or the pool but in local newsrooms where I but worked as an intern at Detroit radio and television stations. I wouldn't settle for sitting behind a desk and answering the phones or getting coffee, as was the case with many a student intern. I knew that was a waste of precious time. I convinced the news directors to let me assist the reporters in any way I could. I took my own notebook along on live shots and press conferences and wrote my own version of stories and then asked reporters and producers to critique them for me.

This personal drive paid off in a big way when one of the anchor-reporters for the then CBS affiliate took a liking to me and allowed me to help her with a series she was doing for the Republican

Party's National Convention. It was being held in Detroit during the summer of 1980. I ended up tagging along for interviews with major politicians, including the Michigan governor, and snagging extra press credentials for the actual GOP convention. This allowed me to watch much of the local and national coverage right from the convention floor! Another professional feat, early on, that propelled me forward.

He ennobled the marriage in Cana of Galilee by his presence, and made it memorable by the first of the miracles which he wrought and for this reason, even from that day forth, it seemed as if the beginning of new holiness had been conferred on human marriages.

Pope Leo XIII, Arcanum

Interesting enough, journalism students at my university were not allowed to apply for internships until completing their sophomore year. I used my Italian version of what my Jewish friends call "chutzpa" to get around the rules. By the time I graduated with my journalism degree in 1981, I had completed three internships and was named the "CMU Outstanding Journalism Graduate." I think you're getting the picture of just how intense, passionate, and driven I was about my chosen profession. Passion, intensity, and drive can be positive attributes but Type-A personalities such as mine must learn to keep them in check, or they can easily overtake all aspects of one's life.

Imagine my surprise when I met my future husband just two weeks after college graduation! That should have been some indication that God was still in the Master Control room, directing my life. I was introduced to Dominic through my brother in-law at their company baseball game. I took one look at the handsome Italian-American man and knew that my opinion about marriage would soon change. We went on our first date in May of 1981 and by December of that year we were engaged.

Dom was different than most of the guys I dated in college. He was not threatened by my strong career ambitions; as a matter of fact, he said that was what had first attracted him to me. He wanted to marry someone whom he could help take care of but who could also take care of herself. Someone who had her own ideas and opinions. An electrical engineer, with a unique specialty in lighting design, he graduated at the top of his class at Penn State University and was recruited by a major architectural engineering firm. He was also very career oriented, like me, and put in a lot of extra hours at the office. Like mine, his own professional perseverance brought him success and allowed him to move into management positions fairly quickly.

Meanwhile, in the first few years of our marriage I was getting recognized for my work in Detroit radio news. It was after receiving several awards from the Associated Press and the "Outstanding Female On Air Award" from the "American Women in Radio and Television" that local television stations started to take notice. One station in particular, which aired the only 10PM news in town, was looking to expand its news staff and offered me a full-time TV reporting position. I, of course, jumped at the chance since it wasn't often that radio newscasters can make the switch to television in such a large market. This was my opportunity for the brass ring and I had no intention of letting that opportunity pass me by.

Several months after I was hired I was offered a switch to the night shift. This had many exhilarating ramifications including live reporting five nights a week, and fill-in anchoring. On the other hand, it also would mean seeing my husband only on the weekends. Dominic and I both saw this as another great opportunity that would give me even more exposure and lead to bigger and better things. We discussed the schedule change and possible conflicts only briefly. We promised each other that we would have "quality time" on the weekends and that I would do my best to visit him at the office during the week for lunch. Everything would be just ducky, we thought. Certainly *we* could handle this.

We soon found out we were not equipped at all to handle the choice we made. Why is it that we are willing to work on almost every other aspect of our lives but think our marriages and our other important relationships will just some how magically take care of themselves? We work hard to gain the experience that will help us land that big promotion. We put in hours at the gym and pay close attention to what we eat and drink in order to maintain a healthy lifestyle. We are willing to put in back-breaking hours of blood, sweat, and tears to have the nicest house on the block. But when it comes to relationships, especially marriage, we somehow have come to believe that it is all supposed to fall in place. In our case, the lack of attention led to our marriage very nearly falling apart.

I soon learned that my new position was much more demanding than I had ever envisioned. A fire or a barricaded gunman story, for example, required the news team to stay on the scene after the newscast ended and be there to catch all the developments on tape. That meant your shift often extended until the wee hours of the following morning as you camped out, waiting. This became a semi-regular occurrence that left me little time for anyone or any thing else for that matter. But I kept going back for more. In the news business you're only as good as your last story and heaven forbid I should miss a scoop. I might lose some of the precious ground I had worked so hard to gain. If it wasn't a breaking story, it was the frequent late nights out with the gang that added to an already long day. Again, I couldn't risk losing business relationships and so was obligated to join the gang every time the gang went out.

I wasn't the only one, however, putting in extra hours. Dominic was given more responsibility at the office and also worked many weekends. We rarely saw each other and when we did it seemed that instead of trying to enjoy the little time we had together we argued constantly. I was very selfish at the time but certainly didn't see it that way. I wanted to be able to do my thing during the week and on the weekends I saw nothing wrong with going to another party or social function that would also help keep my "it" girl reputation intact.

He felt I had a double standard; that I thought it was okay for me to burn the candle at both ends for my own career goals, while he was not allowed to do what he needed to do to get ahead. Of course he was right, but I wouldn't have any of that "Truth" on my plate.

The family is the original cell of social life.

CCC #2207

Getting piled on top of all else was a heaping mound of resentment. We had always been good about dividing up many of the mundane household tasks such as laundry, food shopping, and cleaning. Now, neither of us was living up to our end of the bargain. The neglected responsibilities led to more arguing, blaming, and finger pointing. It became a tit for tat situation. I did this, so now it is your turn to do that. During this difficult time we caused one another a great deal of pain.

Despite how bad things can and did get, as I explained earlier, if you are open, God will bring certain people into your life and use them as ministers of grace to lead you back to Him. It is in this state of brokenness that God is able to work His miracles. God will also work with you and meet you where you are at, even at the most unlikely places and events. In our case He used my obsession with the limelight to start our journey home which began, believe or not, at a Detroit Piston's basketball game.

Tickets to Piston's basketball games back in the early 90's were hot items as the team won back to back NBA Championships in 1989 and 1990. Although seats were difficult to obtain, occasionally members of the news media were invited to games. I was thrilled when my news director told me that one of her friends, a local anchor man, had given her his prized, and near front, seats. The news director was hoping we could join her and her husband for an upcoming Sunday night game. Of course I answered "absolutely" without even checking with Dom first. I could have cared less about the game itself. I was much more interested in the fact that I would be sitting in the VIP section and being "seen" by the local paparazzi. Certainly Dom would be on board with this exciting opportunity that had come my way.

When I told Dom he was upset that another part of our coveted weekends would be spent in shop talk. But, bless his heart, he knew it was important to me. Like everyone in the Detroit area at the time, he was a basketball fan and wisely decided it was better than staying at home and fighting. Providentially, my news director was married to a very talented radio producer and writer who also happened to be an on-fire Christian. I sat next to my boss, half chatting with her and half looking around to see who was looking at me. Meanwhile, Dom sat next to my boss's husband "John," who happened to be a strong evangelical Christian. I had worked in radio with John years earlier and admired his great talent as a producer and writer. I later heard something about him becoming a Christian and getting very involved with the local Salvation Army but didn't give it much thought.

The Holy Spirit worked mightily through John that Sunday night, as he sensed something was not quite right with Dom. John invited

Dom to a weekly men's Bible study and Dom immediately said, "Sure, I'd like to come." As my husband will tell you, when John mentioned the Bible study Dom felt something stir inside and knew that he had to say yes. This is very unusual for Dominic because he is more of an introvert and, as an engineer, he is also very analytical by nature. It takes him a while to process things and make a decision. He isn't one to jump into anything let alone a Bible study. I always tease him that it takes him five years to buy a shirt! Just as the statue of Jesus is beneath my pillow, so was the hand of God at work, courtside, at the Palace of Auburn Hills, Michigan that night.

That Bible study literally changed, then saved, our lives. John gently brought Dom along into an inter-denominational program with Catholics and Protestants. No one ever pressured Dominic to leave the Catholic Church, which can sometimes happen in these types of settings, but they did encourage him to study Scripture and learn more about his faith. When Dom joined the study group, the men were reading about the Old Testament prophets.

It was through the Old Testament that Dominic recognized the roots of the Catholic Church. It brought him back to his days as an altar boy and helped him to better understand, as we like to say, "The wonderful smells and bells of being Catholic." It all made sense to him now; the liturgy, the vestments, the candles, and especially the Eucharist. My husband was so excited that he started going back to Mass regularly and began taking classes at Sacred Heart Major Seminary in Detroit.

As often happens with newfound passion, the recipient can become overzealous. So it was that at first Dominic became very heavy handed with me. This new "Christian thing" of his seemed strange and in some ways frightening. I also felt he saw himself as spiritually superior and saw me as a Christian project. He kept talking about getting back to Church as a couple and saying that we needed to pray together. I didn't know quite what to make of it all and basically told him that we should both be free to do what we each wanted to do faith-wise. He shouldn't judge me, and vice versa.

I also reminded him that the last thing we needed was something else to fight about. Dom backed off and later we would both purposely recall this stage in our faith lives to remind ourselves that evangelization means, as St. Peter reminds us in 1 Peter 3:15, to *always be ready give a defense for the hope that is within you, but to do it with gentleness and reverence.* Hitting someone over the head with the Bible and the Catechism, we learned, doesn't work.

Dominic backed off quite a bit but, unbeknownst to me, continued actively working on me spiritually, behind the scenes so to speak. He brought everything to the Lord in prayer and also asked his Bible study friends to pray for me as well. He was also seeking out other faith based resources on his own. Years later, after our marriage was long on the road to recovery, I would find a beautiful little Christian booklet in Dom's desk entitled, *How to Save Your Marriage Alone.* It made me cry at the time I discovered it. The thought of it still brings me to my knees in gratitude for the graces and mercy of God. What a gift from God to have such a faithful and faith filled husband.

For a while, though, our situation got much worse before it got better. This is often what happens when we commit, or recommit, to Christ and why it is so important not to give up or to give in! Spiritual warfare is real and takes place, especially in the area of Christian evangelization.

Dominic's demeanor, meanwhile, became much more peaceful. He still expressed his concerns but did so in a much less accusatory manner while also taking on more responsibility at home. His loving and sacrificial approach made me uncomfortable and self-conscious. John 3:20 tells us *everyone who does evil hates the light and will not come into the light for fear that his deeds will be exposed.* It felt as if my husband's very presence in our home was shining this burning spotlight on me, exposing all of my ugliness. I didn't like the turmoil in our marriage but I was still too selfish to take a good long look at myself.

If I had done what Dominic had done, and exposed myself to that examination, I might be forced to change. The pressure on me became so intense that we separated briefly. The night I packed my bags and headed out the door to a local hotel, Dom knelt in prayer beside our bed asking the Lord to protect me and bring me back to him. He was worried that I was headed for self-destruction, and he was right. As he climbed into bed he said he felt this huge sense of peace and knew somehow, some way I would come home and our marriage would be healed.

In order, however, that amongst men of every nation and every age the desired fruits may be obtained from this renewal of matrimony, it is necessary, first of all, that men's minds be illuminated with the true doctrine of Christ regarding it; and secondly, that Christian spouses, the weakness of their wills strengthened by the internal grace of God, shape all their ways of thinking and of acting in conformity with that pure law of Christ so as to obtain true peace and happiness for themselves and for their families.

Pope Pius XI, CC

After a few weeks, I moved back home. The separation made me realize that I still loved my husband deeply and wanted to work things out. I didn't know quite how that was going to happen since at the time, I still had no intention of making major changes. I wasn't exactly crazy about all this "church stuff," but I wanted to give our marriage another try. I still wanted it all, just like the commercials promised, where I could bring home the bacon AND fry it up in the pan! It wasn't going to happen, though, as long as I was immersed in the increasingly demanding and highly secular culture of a television newsroom.

It may sound strange, but I am so grateful that I was fired. I was, of course, not happy about it at the time and very bitter toward the powers that be at the TV station, but now there is only gratitude for the suffering, which was crucial for my self-examination and redemption.

My time at the TV station brought us back in touch with my colleague John, whom the Lord used mightily in our faith journey. It was his wife who would eventually make the decision not to renew my contract. Just go ahead and try to wrap your mind about that one! A very strange set of circumstances no doubt, but just another sign that God is God and we are not. This differentiation is said most eloquently in Isaiah 5:8...*my thoughts are not your thoughts, neither are your ways my ways declares the Lord.*

Along with so many other priceless lessons, my work there also revealed negative tendencies and habits that I needed to avoid in the future. This knowledge would help me establish some badly needed professional boundaries. It also gave me additional on-air experience that would benefit me in the years to come.

Some people, and I was definitely one of them, must be stripped of everything in order to be reached. The firing provided, for me, my time in the desert where, as it says in Hosea 2:14 that God speaks to our heart. To speak to our heart means that our heart has to belong to Him. At that point in time I didn't hear His voice. I couldn't hear His voice. My heart had belonged to my career and my career ambitions. God's voice was drowned out by my pangs of confusion, loneliness, and frustration.

Indeed, for months I pounded the pavement for a job, and then pounded my fists in frustration. I was still way too focused on myself. God is a gentleman, however, and He won't sit in the director's chair unless we invite Him to, and that is not done through one prayer but a daily walk with Jesus. I believe it is imperative for us to understand that God is not a puppet master pulling our strings. It is all about relationship. He will direct our paths, if we use our free will to welcome Him into our hearts and our lives. For me that very first move in the right direction took place one day while I was sitting on the edge of our bed, crying.

I was talking out loud and directing my pain toward the crucifix hanging on the wall.

> *Okay Lord. I know I've messed up. If you are the Jesus I met when I made my First Holy Communion, please take the wheel. Please come back into my life. I will do whatever is necessary and whatever you want. If you want me to stay home, that's fine. If you want me to still use my talents in the news business, that's fine too. Just take over because I can't take this anymore.*

My cry for help was music to the Lord's ears. After my literal "come to Jesus" moment, I felt great relief and my attitude about my circumstances slowly started to change. I made a re-commitment to Christ and my Catholic faith, and agreed to seek out help for our marriage problems. When I finally started to listen I realized the Lord was speaking to me in many different ways and through many different people. He spoke to me through a gentle, loving husband who, although wanting greatly to talk about our marriage, instead spent hours allowing me to vent and then provided badly needed words of affirmation.

Jesus spoke to me through the wives of Dominic's Bible study classmates who said they were praying for me. He spoke to me in people I never thought were my friends; the reporters and news photographers and editors who went to bat for me in other newsrooms, helping me find new work. It was definitely a process; one that slowly melted my hardened heart allowing me to finally say "uncle" and turn the Master Control back over to God. My heart would now be able to hear His voice, even just a whisper; my heart was prepared.

Along the way, there were many of those "Aha!" moments, including when we began to realize just how providential the meeting at the Piston's game really was for us. Months later we learned that we were the last couple on the list to be invited. There was a time I would have felt slighted by this, but in retrospect it was simply another detail in God's Master Plan. The other couples had things "suddenly" come up and we were the only two available that night. Coincidence? As my friend John would say, "I think not."

I was grateful for the answered prayers, especially the answer that came in the form of a job offer from a major network affiliate in town. This was amazing to me since the last time I spoke with the news director at this station he had indicated that nothing was available. All of a sudden, though, there seemed to be a newfound interest in my work, and this affiliate wanted to give me a try.

Dom and I actually spent some time praying and talking about the prestigious job offer. I didn't jump for the offer and expect Dom to support my decision. Together we turned to the Lord with the offer. We knew that being the new kid on the block, or the little fish in the big news pond, would most likely mean odd hours and more weekends. We both came to the conclusion that the job offer was a sign that the Lord still wanted to use me in the secular media. We were determined, with God's help, not to make the same mistakes over again. We were committed to the marriage healing process, and committed to growing together as Christians worshipping in the Catholic Church.

I took the job at the local network affiliate. Things were looking up, and I thought most of the challenges were behind us. Little did I know we had many more challenges to face – and the real work was just beginning!

CHAPTER FIVE
"Interrupted Feedback"

I FB, or "interrupted feedback," can be a real help to the reporter in the field (or a real hindrance, depending on the situation). When doing live remotes, it is crucial to be able to hear the cues from the director in the control room. Those cues inform the reporter as to how much time he or she has before the piece goes live. The feedback through the earpiece includes programming, so the reporter knows what is airing before her segment, and hears the anchor's introductions.

The IFB is supposed to smooth transitioning in live programming. However, there are times when reporters, myself included, literally take the IFB out of their ears on camera before the live audience. The cause varies; it could be as simple as a poor signal that makes it difficult to hear anything but static, or a director giving cues that conflict with what the reporter had been told by the executive producer. Removing the earpiece blocks out the distractions and allows the reporter to concentrate on the story.

> *But when he comes, the Spirit of truth, he will guide you to all truth.*
>
> John 16:13a

Since my husband and I had been through some fairly trying times, and both ultimately responded to the still small voice of the Lord with our "yes" to Christ, the Church, and our marriage, I thought that would mean smooth sailing ahead with little interference, static, or mixed signals. I was certain that once I started my new job and we returned to the normal day-to-day routine of married life, my personal IFB was going to be as clear as a bell.

Don't get me wrong. I figured there would be some adjustments to make as Dom and I went to counseling, grew in our faith, and I went back to the business of news reporting. But I was convinced that the Lord had planted me in secular media for good, and that the major hurdles were now behind us. We had put in our time, the future appeared bright and carefree.

I viewed this period of my life as a destination, not as part of a journey. This is where I wanted to be: back in the arms of Jesus and my husband, and back on the air, this time at one of the most prominent network affiliates in the country. I really believed that I would stay in television news forever. I didn't realize that when you are serious about putting God back in the Master Control room, you'd better be ready for a lot of "interrupted feedback." As I had so often done as a reporter, I snatched out that earpiece time and time again, trying to desperately stick to my version of the story.

Many people ask me how long it took to turn my marriage and my life around. They look somewhat stunned when I explain that it took not a few months but several years of hard work, prayer, and daily discernment. It is a never-ending process that continues to this day.

God is persistently working with us to help us be the best we can be while serving Him in this world, so we can "be with Him in the next," as stated in the *Baltimore Catechism.*

Sometimes this "working out our salvation in fear and trembling," as St. Paul encourages us to do in Philippians 2:12, is a pretty tough sell in today's instant gratification society. We want the answers to our troubles ***right now,*** and we want to know that those answers are going to address and solve the problems quickly so we can get on with our lives. After all, we've got our own agendas to pursue, even when we ***feel*** as if we are serving God.

Our media saturated culture has given us all the wrong images and ideas of real life, even in the guise of so called "Reality TV." We are inundated with these shows that are anything but *"real."* Production-wise we have come to learn that even these shows can often be highly scripted, or orchestrated, from behind the scenes.

Even though enlightened by him in whom it believes, faith is often lived in darkness and can be put to the test.

CCC #164

This isn't to say that there aren't a few positive exceptions such as "Extreme Makeover Home Edition" on ABC. For the most part, however, these "reality" programs rarely provide viewers with an uplifting message or useful information that will help them cope with the major issues in their lives, especially in the areas of faith and family. Thanks to the Jack Kevorkians of the world, who push their culture-of-death agenda, suffering is viewed as having no redeeming value. Suffering, our society says, needs to be eliminated, or at least minimized.

This is one of those negative influences, or lies, that had quietly become part of my world, my beliefs. At this point in my life I was not mature enough in my faith, nor was I familiar with terms such as "redemptive suffering." The idea that pain could be used for the gain of God's Kingdom was foreign to me. To suggest that suffering could somehow be embraced and even provide reward was ludicrous. How could a person, through suffering, have a fruitful life?

The greatest act of redemptive suffering, of course, was our Lord's intense death on the cross. The greatest evil committed in the world also turned out to be the salvation of the entire world. Put more simply, there is no Easter Sunday without Good Friday. All of us can point to difficult times that made us stronger or even changed our lives completely. A Bible study instructor of mine used to quote an Arab proverb: "All sunshine makes a desert." Fr. John Hardon's *Modern Catholic Dictionary* explains the purpose of suffering:

> *It is not only to expiate wrongdoing but to enable the believer to offer God a sacrifice of praise of his divine right over creatures, to unite oneself with Christ in his suffering as an expression of love, and in the process to become more like Christ, who having joy set before him, chose the Cross."*

The *Catechism* notes how suffering in this life at times may seem to contrast with what is promised in Scripture:

> *The world we live in often seems very far from the one promised us by faith. Our experiences of evil and suffering, injustice and death seem to contrast with the Good News; they can shake our faith and become a temptation against it. It is then we must turn to the witnesses of faith; to Abraham, who "in hope, believed against hope," to the Virgin Mary, who in her pilgrimage of faith, walked into the "night of faith" in sharing the darkness of her son's suffering and death and to many others: "Therefore, since we are surround by so great a cloud of witnesses let us also lay aside every weight and sin which clings so closely, and let us run with perseverance the race that is set before us looking to Jesus the pioneer and perfecter of our faith (CCC #164-165).*

So many Christians give up when they are about to make a breakthrough. They allow their anger toward their circumstances or problems to control them and then turn that anger toward God instead of turning it *over* to God. Just at the crucial moment when it is imperative to ask for His guidance as to how He wants to turn any given situation into something redemptive, we abandon Him. Or we make the mistake of believing that the "suffering bill" has been paid, due to experiences X, Y, and Z, and that the pain deposited in the "heavenly bank account" makes us home free.

Newsflash! We live in a fallen and imperfect world. This is Catholicism 101 and somehow, in my zeal to start anew, I had forgotten one of the basics I learned in Catholic grade school. It was apparently time for a refresher course.

All suffering stems from original sin. Sometimes we suffer because original sin manifests itself through the poor decisions of others. Many times, as in my own life, suffering is a result of our own bad choices. I never stopped to think about the healing that still needed to take place in my heart, and in my marriage, because of wrong choices I made. I never stopped to think of the long-term redemptive suffering or cleansing that had to occur because of that sin. I learned it was a daily process.

Dom and I would have our good days and our bad days. We had to work slowly through the hurt and the resentment. We also had to work at rebuilding trust. My new position was going quite well. I was getting some top assignments. The station sent me to cover the investigation of the Oklahoma City bombing and then a few months later it was off to New York City for the 1995 Papal visit of John Paul II. I was also getting much better at balancing work and family life. It helped to have a news director who was married with several children. He did his best to be fair regarding holiday and weekend shifts.

Despite the positive signs at the office, Dominic was still skeptical and constantly worried about me once again diving head first into my career. In so many ways Dom knew me better than I knew myself, and he was concerned that I would allow my passion for news to consume me all over again. When I absolutely had to work odd hours, I was afraid to tell him for fear he would give up and go look for some other woman with a "normal" 9 to 5 job. Sometimes our anxieties would lead to terrible arguments, other times silence or avoidance.

Our real healing began with faith formation that we did, for the most part, on our own. We started with what we knew; the Sacraments. We went to Confession and went back to Mass as a couple. When we returned to the Church, in the early to mid 1990's, we didn't have the myriad Catholic resources that exist today: Catholic radio, Catholic websites, and Catholic Bible studies. The burgeoning of these things have been a blessing from the Holy Spirit inspiring men and women to respond to a need within the Catholic community.

Dom and I were aware of EWTN, but our schedules didn't allow for much time in front of the television set. I started studying Scripture through a women's non-denominational Bible study and eventually we joined a couple's study group. Counseling was another step in the right direction, as was signing up for a Marriage Encounter weekend. If you are not familiar with World Wide or National Marriage Encounter, I highly encourage you to visit their web sites at either www.me.org or www.marriage-encounter.org.

The weekends, as the promotional information explains, focus on the "communications between husbands and wives" and offers "a unique approach aimed at revitalizing marriage." These gatherings have a long history of strengthening and renewing thousands of relationships. We also became more involved in our parish and began initiating conversations about Catholicism with our priests and deacons.

Ever so slowly we were stretching ourselves: learning, growing, and praying as a couple. I think the biggest single factor was simply plowing through, minute-by-minute, and refusing to give in to the ups and downs. As my husband likes to say, you don't wake up one day forty pounds overweight. It happens gradually; an extra piece of cake here, a few extra French fries there. The same thing is true with healing a relationship. Our problems compounded themselves over time, and it was childish on my part to think they could be solved overnight.

Scripture says that life is a race to be run with perseverance. In His love and mercy, God provides us with opportunities to show we will diligently pursue Him and His will for our lives.

One Sunday morning after Mass, Dom was reading our parish bulletin and noticed an ad for a parish pilgrimage to the Holy Land. Something told us we needed to go. We love to travel, and we were excited at the prospect of making our Bible studies come alive. This was another one of those newsflashes or turning points.

The pilgrimage was anointed in many ways, and to this day continues to produce much fruit. It was during this first trip to Israel that we started to see the depth and history of the Catholic Church. One young man who was on the trip with us was inspired to pursue the priesthood. We formed many friendships that are still strong thirteen years later, including friendships that brought us into marriage ministry at our parish.

The engaged couples program was a six-week mandatory course taught by married couples in the parish, along with several talks and sessions with the pastor. Two of the women from the program were fellow pilgrims on our Holy Land trip; they invited us to an upcoming ministry meeting. Dom and I were looking for a way to express our gratitude to God for saving our marriage, and we thought this would be a good place to start.

At this point we were married for just over twelve years. New leadership couples were given all the materials to review and were asked to help out with minor tasks before actually delivering any presentations. We were half thrilled and half irate at what we began learning about the Sacrament of Marriage. The Church teachings were so beautiful, we wondered why we hadn't heard this before. We were in our mid-to-late 30s, and were now just discovering that husbands and wives are called to help each other get to heaven.

With reason, therefore, does the Sacred Council of Trent solemnly declare: "Christ Our Lord very clearly taught that in this bond two persons only are to be united and joined together when He said: 'Therefore they are no longer two, but one flesh'."

Pope Pius XI, CC

No one had ever told us that marriage signifies the union of Christ and His Church, with Christ being the Bridegroom and the Church being the Bride. We may have heard the Scripture readings concerning these teachings at a Catholic wedding or Mass, but the theology behind them had never been explained beyond a short homily, so we never gave them much thought. We volunteered with the engaged couples program for several years, and gained much knowledge concerning the Church teachings on marriage and family. These teachings encouraged and challenged us, and sent this one-time former Catholic rebel back to the confessional again and again!

Meanwhile, I thought we were on the right track. We were working hard on our marriage, giving back to the Church, and trying to grow in our faith. That's why I was so surprised when the interrupted feedback started coming through. I couldn't believe what I was hearing. Why was I getting such confusing and conflicting messages all of a sudden about the news business and the media in general? Where were these unsettling questions coming from? The signals or cues couldn't be from God, could they?

After all, the Lord certainly could see how Dom and I were fighting the good fight of faith. We didn't give up on our marriage, despite the daily challenges. I was really trying to honor my commitments by putting faith and family before the office. And even my work reflected my love for the Lord, as I did my best to provide a public service rather than a personal promotion with my news reports.

Why, then, was I noticing an increased sensationalism in our news coverage that made me uncomfortable? Why did the local and national media seem to be buying more and more into the "if it bleeds it leads" adage? Why was I covering more storms, fires, car crashes, and shootings, and producing fewer investigative type stories on politics and education? And was it just me, or was there a real chill coming through the newsroom whenever I would raise concerns about liberal media bias when it came to stories concerning religion, especially the Catholic Church? Then, the most frightening thoughts popped into my head: Could God possibly be asking me to leave the secular media? That was the first time the IFB connecting me to God's Master Control room was yanked out of my ear. *There is no way the Lord would ask me that,* I thought. *You're just stressed or a little burned out from all the stuff you've had to deal with in the last few years,* I told myself repeatedly.

This is what happens when you draw closer to the Lord. The Lord will start revealing Truths to you. This interrupted feedback, or Godly communication, doesn't necessarily happen at Mass or while you're doing the daily readings or saying your prayers. God speaks to us at all different times and in many different ways. He speaks to us through what we know. I don't know much about a lot of things, but I do know the news business, and so it makes sense that the Lord chooses to speak to me through personal encounters or experiences at work.

There were many God-moments that are still fresh in my memory, even though they happened more than a decade ago. These were additional newsflashes or bulletins that propelled me to really begin to address the vocation questions I was hearing deep in the recesses of my heart. One particularly poignant newsflash centers on a train wreck I was covering. I was sent to do a follow-up story about one of the young victims, who was killed while riding in a car that tried to beat an on-coming train. Several other people in the car had been killed, and the wreck had injured a number of other people as well. The station wanted me to talk to the teen's family to see if I could get some fresh comments on tape for the 11PM news.

When I hopped in the news van with my photographer, we looked at each other and rolled our eyes. "Here we go again. More blood, guts, and tears," I said. Talking to grieving family members is one of the worst aspects of the news business, and photographers dislike it as much as the reporters do. Having to shine a spotlight or push a bulky, obtrusive camera in the face of someone in the midst of personal grief or tragedy makes a cameraman feel as though he works for a tabloid newspaper or the European paparazzi instead of a legitimate news operation.

Both the cameraman and I agreed that the last thing this poor family needed was another TV news crew rolling into their driveway. We decided we would drive down their street, and then leave. At least we could tell the station we had been to the neighborhood. That was a fine plan except we both forgot that it is near impossible to go unnoticed in a live TV vehicle with call letters painted boldly all over the vehicle. Someone inside the home spotted us, and within seconds a distraught young man ran out of the house, yelling something like, "Leave us alone!" I could see the pain in his eyes, and hear it in his voice. So this is what my journalism career had come to: ambulance chasing.

O God, keep my tongue from evil, and my lips from deceitful speech. Let me know the way I should go, for to You do I lift my soul.

Excerpt from a Yom Tov Silent Prayer

The quote from John Paul II came to mind: *The service of humanity through the medium of truth is something worthy of your best years, your finest talents, your most dedicated efforts...* Was I serving humanity through the medium of truth by chasing them down and asking them "how they feel" about their son or brother getting killed? The news audience already had more than enough information about this tragedy. It was pretty obvious that what I was serving was sensationalism and the thirst for higher ratings. That's when I decided I better put the earpiece back in and start talking back to the Master Controller. But here's a warning; don't try this at home unless you are ready for some real challenges.

My soul searching led to many tearful and frustrating moments between me and God. I knew the business was changing; the business I loved was now very different. I wasn't the only one who felt it. The conversation with the photographer was just one of many I had with newsroom colleagues and friends of mine who worked in other news outlets around the country. So much was changing in our industry. Cable, the Internet, and other sources of news, information, and entertainment combined with busy lifestyles meant viewers had other choices. No longer were they necessarily pulling up to the dinner table and turning on the local evening news.

As a result, stations felt they had to do more with less to get, and keep, the attention of the audience. That is why there was such an increase in coverage of crime and violence. Sad but true. It is cheap and easy to cover and very plentiful, especially in major cities. Remember, we live in a fallen and imperfect world. A world filled with news that catches the viewer's interest, at least for a moment, and thus captures ratings. Mr. and Mrs. Smith will watch to make sure the explosion or gas leak is not in their neighborhood and then they grab the remote and move on to something else. The stations, often at the national level, kept pushing the sensational envelope in hopes of getting that viewer back. There was really very little that local management could do against this insatiable appetite for sensational news. It quickly became a blur, a chicken and egg situation. Did the viewers really want more or did supplying more addict the viewers? And if a local station bucked the trend, they'd be gone. Their very existence was at stake. The industry was losing its soul and all for the sake of ratings and profits. The addicted viewer was now a necessary casualty in the ratings war.

These revelations about the industry that I loved so dearly, and sacrificed so much for, were heartbreaking for me to accept. One night, while waiting for Dom to come home, I was preparing dinner and decided to have it out with God. As I cut vegetables for salad, I started shouting out to the Lord through my tears: "I don't understand why this is happening. Why is my business changing, and why did you put me back on the air? You're God and you know everything. And if you knew this was going to happen, well why in the world would you want me to go through this? Is this some cruel joke you're playing on me? Haven't I proved to you that I love you and am committed to you? What in the world am I supposed to do now? I don't know how to do anything else! You gave me these talents, so now you have to give me some answers here, Lord!"

What happened next stopped me in my tracks. I was alone in the house. Besides the sound of my sniffling, there was complete silence. No TV or radio playing in the background. Of course, I wasn't alone at all. Jesus was right there. So much so that I heard Him speak to me. "I can't use you in the secular media anymore."

I dropped the knife and started looking around the kitchen, half expecting to see Jesus at the other end of the counter or behind me sitting at the table. The voice was that clear. I kept asking more questions. "Okay, but where? And how are you going to use me? How will I know?"

The silence returned. No more cues or interrupted feedback coming from Master Control. Instead I stood there in my kitchen waiting and wondering what the next assignment would be.

PLEASE STAND BY:
A PHRASE USED BY A TV OR
RADIO ANNOUNCER TO INFORM
THE AUDIENCE OF A TECHNICAL
DIFFICULTY OR AN
INTERRUPTION IN REGULARLY
SCHEDULED PROGRAMMING

CHAPTER SIX
"Please Stand By"

Don't just do something. Sit there." My colleague at the Catholic television station EWTN, Colleen Carroll Campbell, recently shared this catchy slogan with me. It's a great reminder for the busy bees of this world, those Type-A personalities, to slow down and take badly needed time for relaxation and reflection. And it sounds an awful lot like the advice given to us over and over again in the Bible.

Be still and know that I am God.

Psalm 46:10

I could have used Colleen's sage advice years ago. Spending a lot more time in God's word also would have helped before I did the old Tomeo "damn the torpedoes-full speed ahead" routine for which I had become famous. But the words "patience," "waiting," "be still," or "please stand by" were not, as you might have already guessed, popular words in my vocabulary. They were for people willing to let life, and all its trappings, pass them by; and I wasn't one of those people!

Wait for the Lord; be strong and take heart and wait for the Lord.

Psalm 27:14

But if we hope for what we do not yet have, we wait for it patiently.

Romans 8:25

I was angry at God again. Each new plateau seemed to find me digging deeper within myself and resulted in even more anger. This time it was because I felt *I* had followed through with what I was supposed to do but *He* wasn't living up to *His* end of the bargain. Weren't we, He and I, partners? Didn't I have as much control as He did? Obviously, I still had some ego issues to deal with. I mean, honestly, who in the world was I to question and challenge the Almighty Creator of the universe? This is just another of the countless signs that illustrate to me the unending mercy of God. After all, if I were in charge I would have zapped me right then and there based on the arrogance alone. But then again, that's why God is God and, thank goodness, we are not.

Once again, I didn't sit around waiting and wondering for very long. I yanked out that IFB and decided that I would take matters into my own hands. I would show God that I still belonged in the secular media. "Teresa Tomeo" was a fixture in the Detroit broadcasting market, and I wasn't about to let that change. How could the Lord not understand that my presence was still needed on the airwaves of the Motor City? Sure the business seemed to going down the proverbial drain, but maybe it was just a phase.

Yes, I was getting burned out and tired of the meaningless TV news chatter, but I was strong. Yes, I was exhausted from all the ratings hype, but I could handle it. But the still, small voice inside, the one that I had earnestly learned to listen to, appropriately whispered, "Hmmm, Mrs. Smarty Pants, didn't you mutter those same words about your 'emotional handling' capabilities at another crucial stage in your life that began on the unemployment line? Aren't you forgetting what happened after that?"

I quickly put those questions out of my mind. In hindsight, they were, no doubt, some form of a prompting from the Holy Spirit (okay, maybe minus the "Mrs. Smarty Pants" part), but then I soon came up with what I thought was the perfect solution. You know, sort of like on the silver screen: Dorothy heads back to Kansas. She gets it, that she had it all along. Or Scarlet in the last scene of *Gone with the Wind.* She believes going back to Tara, her original family home, would solve all her problems. It seemed almost painfully obvious what should happen: Teresa Tomeo would go back to her original broadcasting home, radio.

It appeared to be the perfect solution. I could stay in broadcasting without having my Catholicism and my journalism ethics continually challenged, or so I thought. There is a wonderful line in the opening scene of the movie *Bella.* In it, the narrator says, "My grandmother always said, 'If you want to make God laugh, tell Him your plans.'" So here I was, formulating plans and sharing them with God. Certainly He wanted my input. Clearly He would realize that I could have my cake and eat it, too. Boy, was I in for another rude awakening.

Woe to the rebellious children, says the Lord, who carry out plans that are not mine.

Isaiah 30:1

Dominic knew I was disillusioned with the television news end of my business and just wanted me to be happy. I decided to accept a position, which would be my last full-time job in the secular media, at one of the large FM radio stations in Detroit. I had actually worked there very early on in my career as a part-time newsperson, and now I was offered the news director's job. It meant early mornings, the very wee hours of the morning. But I would be part of the coveted morning drive slot. My responsibilities included news twice an hour. I also served as one of the "side-kicks" for the morning show host. The pay was great, the station was doing fairly well in the ratings, and the best part was I could leave at noon.

Although the newscasts were relatively short (two to three minutes long), I was also responsible for recording a 30 minute weekly public affairs show that allowed me to continue to serve the listeners at least some degree of in-depth coverage of important topics. The icing on that cake was the fact that these pieces included many segments dedicated to events in the local Christian community. My world would go on with me trying to serve both the god of the news world and the God of my faith.

Over the course of this two-year stint, I went to great lengths to convince myself that I could keep one foot in the secular world and one foot in the Christian world. But I simply could not serve two masters. The industry had changed, and I had changed. Even though I tried to fit in, I no longer could. There was an unsettling feeling deep down that would not go away. Dom and I were still doing all of the religious activities; going to Bible study, remaining active in the parish, and trying to learn more about the Church. Our marriage continued to heal but my heart was heavy. I knew that I was drowning out the voice of God because I was so afraid of what I might hear.

The same phenomenon that impacted the quality of TV news was also occurring up and down the AM and FM radio dials. There was more competition that eventually led to the shock jock genre so prevalent in radio programming today. Slowly, the morning host at my station was being pressured to increase the sleaze factor. The big broadcasting conglomerates were getting bigger and buying up more radio properties. They insisted on doing more with much less.

Nothing was sacred. The bottom line was *the* bottom line; the radio sales department eventually turned my public affairs show into a 30-minute infomercial for potential advertisers. By that time, at the turn of the 21st century, I had worked in the secular media for some twenty years. Twenty years of toil and tears had been boiled down to two minutes of news on an FM station. Again some familiar questions started to surface: What did I have to show for my efforts, and where do I go from here?

A major part of my uneasiness came from trying to come to grips with the downfall of secular media. Deep within, I knew the Lord was trying to show me that there were major problems in the mass media and entertainment industries that needed to be addressed. More and more stories were surfacing about the connections between violence in the media and aggressive behavior in children. It seemed that with just about every school shooting, sooner or later, we would hear about the suspects and their obsession with violent video games and movies.

The Federal Trade Commission was so concerned about this issue that, following the Columbine massacre, the agency started investigating the marketing of violent media products to children. If that weren't enough to show me that I needed to get involved, there were the efforts of Christian and other conservative groups who were starting to voice their concerns about the liberal bias of the press. Organizations such as the Parents TV Council and Focus on the Family were gathering more steam with their grassroots efforts to alert the public to the problems of media influence. Maybe the Lord was trying to show me that my experience as a media insider could be of some help. Part of me wanted to tell everyone the big story about the media. Part of me knew that once I did, I couldn't turn back.

Consider what Jesus tells us in Matthew 16:24-26.

> *If anyone would come after me, he must deny himself and take up his cross and follow me. For whoever wants to save his life will lose it but whoever loses his life for my sake will*

> *find it. What good will it be for a man if he gains the whole*
> *world yet forfeits his soul?*

Hadn't I already come way too close to losing both my marriage and my soul? Every time I tried life on my own terms, there were disastrous results. I knew well what Jesus also tells us in the Gospel of John . . .

> *I am the vine. You are the branches. If a man remains in me*
> *and I in him, he will bear much fruit. Apart from me you*
> *can do nothing* (John 15:5).

However, my heart was not fully accepting the knowledge that my head knew to be true. When I first returned to the Catholic Church, this verse had become near and dear to me. I realized how much I needed to make God the center of my life. Somehow I had forgotten not only this verse, but the other convicting words of Jesus that preceded it:

> *I am the vine, and my Father is the gardener. He cuts off*
> *every branch in me that bears no fruit, while every branch*
> *that does bear fruit He prunes so that it will be even more*
> *fruitful* (John 15:1).

Ouch! I forgot about the pruning part. It hurt, but it was better than the alternative.

My decision to leave the secular media was finalized one morning as I went back to the newsroom after my on air shift. The newspapers arrived late that day and I started to go through them just to kill time before noon rolled around and I could leave. That's when I noticed one of the headlines. *"American Academy of*

Pediatrics Says No TV for Children Under Two." This story was on the front page of a major national newspaper.

The AAP was advising its members that their youngest patients needed to steer clear of television completely. They encouraged pediatricians to warn the parents of patients about the dramatic effects television viewing could have on children. I knew from my own experience, and other stories that were starting to surface, how bad the media climate was getting; but prior to seeing this alarming report from a major professional organization, I really didn't have the guts to get involved. This was the catalyst that propelled me to put the press badge back on and start digging. I didn't know exactly what I was going to do about the problem but I knew I just couldn't stand by and watch what was happening to the media. It also became impossible for me to make money off of something that conflicted with my moral values and was increasingly becoming a very real threat to society.

I had my new assignment, and I also had a great sense of peace. I wasn't angry with God anymore. The scales were falling from my eyes and I was able to see, with gratitude, how He had been pruning me, preparing me, for work for His kingdom.

I recalled the words of one of my dear friends, a wonderful Protestant preacher who works with the homeless in the inner city. His encouragement came after I poured my frustrations out over the phone to him one day. I told him how confused and disillusioned I had become and that I just didn't know what the Lord wanted me to do with my life anymore.

Teresa, God does not waste His time. It is not clear right now but someday you will see how every aspect of your life will be used for His Glory. Just wait and see.

A few weeks after the AAP story broke, I sat down with the station's general manager. I wasn't sure what to expect when I walked into his office but knew it had to be done. I told him that I could sense that I wasn't meshing into the programming format and I was tired of the struggle. It was clear to me that they were going for a younger and more edgy audience and at 40 years old, I didn't fit the morning drive demographic that was their target.

We had a nice conversation and the exchange helped make for an easy exit. I left on a positive note and with the station buying out the remainder of my contract; I also walked out the door with a smile and a hefty sized check. It wasn't money meant for me, though. It was meant for the furthering of God's call on my life and I used the money to start my own web site and communications company.

> *If anyone would come after me, he must deny himself and take up his cross and follow me. For whoever wants to save his life will lose it but whoever loses his life for my sake will find it. What good will it be for a man if he gains the whole world yet forfeits his soul?* (Mark 8:34-36).

It seemed as if God were now saying to me, "Teresa, are you really willing to lay down your life in the media for Me? Are you willing to take up that Cross and follow Me, even if it means walking away from life in the media as you know it?"

I was being asked to keep my eyes on Him, to follow Him with trust and confidence. Being a woman who had always been "in charge" I could see how this was an important step for my relationship with God. He needed to know I would accept as much as I needed to accept.

"Yes, Lord," I was finally able to say with peace and conviction in my heart, "wherever You take me, here I am. I have come to do Your will."

CHAPTER SEVEN
"Segue"

The idea of being a business owner or starting my own communications company was never even a blip on my radar screen. So why was the segue, or transition, from secular anchor to an entirely different vocation going so smoothly? Why did the process feel so natural?

This can be best explained by the promise of the Lord in St. Matthew's Gospel. *His* yoke is easy and *His* burden light. Back in Jesus' day the people would be able to relate to this analogy. They were peasants and hardworking farmers, familiar with regularly yoking their own animals with the wooden bar or frames to help carry loads or plow the fields.

Come to me,
all you who are weary
and burdened,
and I will
give you rest.
Take my yoke
upon you
and learn from me,
for am I gentle
and humble in heart
and you will find rest
for your souls.
For my yoke is easy
and my burden
is light.

Matthew 11:25-30

Jesus uses the imagery of carrying a burden to illustrate how any yoke placed upon you by God is not going to weigh you down spiritually or emotionally. The yokes of Christ are not too great of a burden to bear on our own. After all, they aren't our own but are given with great love and mercy for our growth. Christ willingly accompanies us to help us carry our burden.

Indeed, the Lord's yoke doesn't strain at the neck, back and shoulders, or crush the spirit. Instead, it's a perfect fit. Dominic related a Bible commentary he once read about this passage, and it really illuminated this specific teaching for me. The writer explained that yokes were constructed for the individual animal so the animal would be comfortable and not fight the piece of equipment. The better the fit, the more efficiently and quickly they finished the tasks.

This analogy can easily apply to our lives if we can learn to submit to the yoke of God. He has a plan for us, and if we accept that plan or yoke and live in God's will we will be happier, and much more at peace.

For me, and for most people, the key word was and is ***submission***. I needed to submit my will completely to God and show Him that I was ready to entrust myself fully to whatever He had in store for me. This included my marriage and my career. The longer I fought the Lord, the more I felt like a square peg trying to push myself into a small round hole. That's why, even though I was still "in my element," so to speak, as a radio news director; I felt uneasy, restless, very unsettled and even burdened.

Stop and think about that for a minute. There I was, with years and years of experience in newsrooms and on the air, and yet I felt like I didn't belong. The feeling kept getting stronger and stronger. This "fish out of water" sense seemed to engulf me when I was sent to represent the radio station at a national broadcasting convention. My interests were so far removed from the topic of the panel discussions. The keynote speakers, mostly network news stars, failed to hold my interest. I spent most of the time at this "prestigious" conference in my hotel room or chatting with two very sweet broadcasting students from my Alma Mater, Central Michigan University. At least I had something in common with them.

When I reflect on those last few years in the secular media I can see how I struggled with the yoke placed upon me. Like a new animal that has yet to be yoked, I didn't realize what a perfect fit it was; but, rather, did my best to unburden myself. Thus, in my struggles, the yoke felt heavy and uncomfortable; surely it was dragging me down with its ill-fit and need of adjustment. You can even imagine this scene, as I'm sure you've "been there, done that."

The way of Christ "leads to life;" a contrary way "leads to destruction."

CCC #1696

When I submitted, however, the Lord gently showed me His interest in my well-being, and my own desire in removing the yoke began to subside. Slowly it became obvious to me that this wasn't a burden at all. I was with the Lord, working for Him and filled with gratitude and relief.

In society's eyes, the word "submission" translates into control or oppression. The Christian meaning of the word is just the opposite. Submission to God is true freedom. That's why I felt so at peace with my decision to start my own communications company. It sounds crazy, doesn't it? I had never run a business before. I didn't know exactly what "Teresa Tomeo Communications LLC" would become, or whether the company would ever turn into a viable business that would help support me and my husband, but it really didn't matter. Somehow I knew that God had a plan, and that I would be fine. My trust was placed firmly in the Lord who had so lovingly yoked me to work for His kingdom. It is easy to feel regret that we don't experience our epiphanies a lot sooner, but I have come to embrace the fact that they are part of the journey. That is why they are gifts from God. Those "aha" moments give us clarity and encouragement, and must put a smile upon our Creator's face.

Many people, from colleagues to friends and family, thought I had lost my mind. They shook their heads, wondering how I would get my new company off the ground without having access to the free publicity of the air waves. They didn't realize that I served the God who created the universe. I felt emboldened with the realization that if I lived to serve Him, He would take care of the details. This isn't to say it wasn't a whole lot of hard work and diligence on my part but I figured He would handle helping a little bitty communications operation that was meant for His glory. All it takes is the faith of a mustard seed and God will move mountains.

Dominic and I sat down and discussed a business plan for Teresa Tomeo Communications LLC. He asked me what I hoped to accomplish. "I want to let my misery be my ministry," I told him.

"Wow. That's powerful stuff," he said.

I explained I heard those words from a preacher on a syndicated Protestant radio show, and they made perfect sense to me. I was miserable about what was happening to the media, and I felt called to do something about it. I went on to share with Dom that when I heard the words it forced me to think about all the amazing people I had interviewed over the years who had done the same thing; turned their pain into something positive to help others. There was the Detroit grandmother who was so tired of the gangs and the drug dealers that she formed her own community watchdog group. After just a few months of regular protests in front of the drug infested homes the thugs, who of course wanted to avoid any possible attention, went elsewhere. This elderly woman not only made a difference in her own neighborhood but inspired others to do the same. All the while gaining more police support for inner city residents.

There was another woman who was a victim of domestic violence and decided to fight back by becoming a Christian counselor and working with other abuse victims. This was a woman who wouldn't let her pain go unused.

As a result, those who suffer in accord with God's will hand their souls over to a faithful creator as they do good.

1 Peter 4:19

Then there was the suburban Detroit man who lost a daughter in a horrible drunk driving accident. You could hardly blame him for being bitter. His daughter was an innocent victim. She was not drinking, and was wearing her seatbelt when a drunk driver ran a stop sign and slammed into her vehicle. This grieving father turned his misery into a billboard campaign for the Oakland County Michigan Chapter of Mothers against Drunk Driving. (M.A.D.D. was also started by a woman whose daughter had been killed by a drunk driver, long before drunken driving laws were on the books.) This father chose to harness his hurt in such a way that others might be spared the same. These were only a few of the people I had come to know and admire over the years.

In just a few short minutes I had come up with quite a list of some very special people I had interviewed; they were ordinary folks who did extraordinary things by turning their pain into something positive to help others. They let their misery be their ministry.

"Okay," Dom said. "Now we need to get more specific about what aspects of the media makes you miserable and how your talents can be used to make a difference."

I took his words as marching orders, and went to my home office and started cranking out ideas for talks and presentations. "Making a Difference in the Media" became the title of one of my most popular seminars. I had done quite a lot of public speaking already, as a local media personality. Much of it had been at career seminars and special events. I knew that speaking would be a key component of my ministry. I was exhilarated by the camaraderie between myself and the audience, and thanked God for each opportunity to make presentations to people.

"Making a Difference in the Media" developed into a general media awareness presentation that gave families, and other concerned citizens, a general overview of the media awareness issues plus action items to apply in their homes and in the culture. My in-depth knowledge of the industry was giving me a foundation from which I could offer both a real way to confront what the media does to families, which I did with the action items, but also fueled my passion for my new ministry. In some ways I felt as if I was running ahead of an out-of-control blaze, trying to warn everyone in its path. "Get out of the way! Save yourself! Save your family!" I knew all too well what the industry was about; I couldn't be silent anymore.

I also thought about how negatively I was influenced by the entertainment industry as a young girl. At the age of twelve I tried to model myself after a favorite television star that also happened to be rail thin. The images on the screen and in the magazines combined with the standard peer pressure of that age and resulted in my efforts to slowly starve myself down to 89 pounds. I was diagnosed with anorexia nervosa, an illness that had recently been identified as a serious eating disorder. I say that with a simplicity that belies the complexity of the disorder.

In the early 1970's there was no MTV, no Internet, no satellite television with 250 channels to choose from, no instant messaging, and no cell phones. I think of how these things have added to the dilemmas our younger generation faces and can't help but get on my soapbox! Without the additional images of today, I was still so taken with the media's idea of what I should look like that I wound up in the hospital for over two weeks, and almost missed out on the start of my high school years.

The illness reeked havoc on my young body, which was going through puberty at that time. My periods stopped and there were other medical complications. The medical community didn't know all that much about eating disorders at that time and so the doctors told me to essentially "gain weight or we are going to recommend that your parents keep you out of school for several months." Well, you already know that I didn't let that happen. I did what I had to do and with the help of some very loving parents and a really good pediatrician, I put on some desperately needed pounds and set off for high school and the rest of my life.

But I believe that one never truly gets "over" an eating disorder. In many ways it stays with you. Being a public person, I have to be conscious of the way I look and sometimes I can honestly say that thirty-plus years after anorexia, finding balance can still be a bit of a challenge. I channeled these concerns into another presentation and seminar made available to private and public schools, as well as parishes, and called it "Choices and Challenges Facing Today's Teens."

Often when I was developing ideas for seminars, it felt as if the Holy Spirit took over, as though I was a bystander watching the ministry grow. Ideas would pop into my head and quickly end up in an outline form for another talk. Of all things, I was learning, with each passing day, to be thankful for painful experiences in my past. I was using them, and I was sharing them with others.

Additional areas of the "misery" that I needed to apply to my ministry dealt with media bias, media sensationalism, and media relations. I had witnessed firsthand how those with little experience or inside knowledge could be ignored, mistreated, or manipulated.

Charity is the greatest social commandment. It respects others and their rights.

CCC #1889

One egregious example was the media coverage of a school shooting in Flint Michigan, north of Detroit. The media marched into the town following the shooting death of a five-year-old girl who was killed by another student who had brought a gun to class. Granted, this was a very big story with all sorts of issues that needed to be examined due to the age of the victim and the shooter; but the media was out of control. Some literally pitched tents and camped out near the school. Others offered residents living near the grade school cold hard cash in exchange for permission to use their backyards as base camp for news coverage. I knew that my expertise in covering breaking news stories could help officials deal effectively with crisis situations. There were ways to ensure access and continued coverage for the press while maintaining some sense of decorum and control, especially during a developing story and on-going police investigation.

These issues soon became the basis for my crisis media management seminars. My professional advice as a media consultant proved to be a valuable service to a number of different entities such as school districts, auto plants, and government offices.

The ideas were all there. Dom had been integral to the plan behind the communications company that was now taking root. My next step was to get the word out. The first big break came in the form of a phone call from a friend of mine. She knew that I was no longer in the news business and apparently felt comfortable enough to unload on me. She immediately began complaining about how disgusted she was with the local press. Her community group had great story ideas to share and none of the stations or local papers was interested in anything but car accidents and snow storms. As I had grown to see, they wanted some "breaking news" headline to throw at unsuspecting viewers and listeners to get them to "tune in" for further developments. A pleasant story about a group of homeowners cleaning up their streets wasn't newsworthy.

In turn, I shared with her my own frustrations and how I was working hard to turn the frustrations into a ministry. "Hey," she said. "My group is looking for a keynote speaker for an upcoming meeting. Do you think you could come and talk to us about some of these issues?" I accepted the offer and the talk was a hit. I prayed about how much I would share about the negative media climate and decided that naming names or pointing fingers was not the right thing to do. This was not about my being fired or one lousy news manager or executive. It was about the mass media and entertainment industry that was quickly losing its soul for the sake of the almighty dollar. It was about bringing awareness to the media's very specific agendas. I gave some examples from my own experience and then backed them up with statistics and studies concerning the various aspects of media influence.

Then I provided an insider's perspective on how concerned citizens could challenge and change the media climate. I encouraged the audience to contact broadcast and print media representatives. I explained how effective the personal phone calls and letters really were, and that viewers and listeners should also be communicating with advertisers and program sponsors. Two could play the money game! Everyone was encouraged to boldly file complaints with the FCC if they felt it necessary. I wanted to make sure everyone knew they had power and weren't at the mercy of the industry.

One woman told me I should take the presentation on the road because so many people needed to hear the truth about the media, especially from an "insider." And God bless her, she didn't cringe when she called me that! Someone else suggested I write a book, and yet another person thought that I should have my own radio talk show! All very prophetic statements when you consider how Almighty God has since developed my ministry. And all I did was submit to the yoke and say "yes."

The speaking slowly started to pick up steam while God amazingly continued to work out all the details and bring the right people into my life at the right time. But I can easily look back and say had all the same people been in my life a decade earlier I would have missed the boat, so to speak. This is why I encourage everyone to embrace their journey and see God's hand always at work.

> *You do not possess because you do not ask. You ask but do not receive, because you ask wrongly, to spend it on your passions.*
>
> James 4:2b-3

Dom asked his Bible study for prayers for our new venture and his group leader, Steve, asked if I was going to do a web site. Steve is still a dear friend as well as an associate pastor at a wonderful non-denominational church in the Detroit area. He also owned his own web site development company with another good friend of ours. "Yes," Dom said. "We're looking into it."

We didn't have to look any further because Steve insisted on developing and maintaining my web site for free. Dom had known

Steve's area of expertise, but didn't feel quite right asking for Steve's help. But Steve was serious, he told Dom. He really believed in what I was doing; as a minister, he had seen firsthand the impact the mass media was having on Christian communities.

I almost fell over when Dom came home and told me Steve's offer. This was another major answer to prayer. Anyone who owns a business knows that building a good website is crucial, but it can also be extremely costly. What a gift this was! A Christian brother in the Lord, who also happened to be a web site creator and developer, was going to design and maintain my site for free. Bless Steve's heart and praised be Jesus Christ. Steve took on the task of www.teresatomeo.com for several years and, despite our repeated efforts, would never take any money. I will forever be grateful for his help.

I could probably fill another book with the stories of other angels the Lord sent to me while starting my ministry. There was my friend and former colleague, Mark, the radio sportscaster, a Lutheran brother in the Lord, who had been speaking for years and heard I was starting out on the circuit. He offered great guidance and direction. There were other friends and contacts who played an important role in my segue, including the program director of the local Evangelical station who offered me my very first talk show. We met through a media fellowship group. I didn't know it at the time, but he was slowly converting to Catholicism and would eventually end up hosting a morning show for a Catholic radio apostolate.

At this point, only about three months had passed since I had repeated the big "yes" Lord. Things were moving quickly and the idea of making a ministry out of my media misery was becoming a reality. The opportunity to move the ministry further along came in the form of an offer to host my own midday, one hour talk show.

This was another one of those stunning "aha" moments. I was pretty convinced that walking away from the secular media might mean never returning to the air waves. I told God that I was willing to take up my cross and lose my life as I knew it, "for His sake." In the process, just as He promises, He helped me find "new life."

The talk show on Protestant radio was a real gift, and a time of continued growth and education in my faith. It was great to be back on the air again five days a week, especially to talk about Jesus. My news background was key in my success as I was able to bring years of interviewing experience and a long list of local contacts to the table. The new radio job gave me more confidence to promote my media awareness message. I felt a call to still reach out to the secular world and was able to write an occasional special report on media issues for one of the local daily newspapers. The assignments led to a weekly media column that ran for four years.

My Protestant brothers and sisters at the station reaffirmed my love of Scripture and introduced me to the Protestant community through many functions, all of which helped greatly expand my speaking ministry. There were plenty of challenges from some former, poorly catechized Catholics who did their best to try and "save" me. I know they thought they were doing me a favor; and actually they were, but not in the way they would have anticipated.

Their challenges turned me into a Catholic apologist practically overnight! First up were some of the significant differences between the faiths that revolved around statues, saints, and the Virgin Mary. Of course I knew that we Catholics don't "worship statues or the saints or the Blessed Mother," as they claimed, but I couldn't answer their questions based upon Scripture. This, even though I had been in Bible study for sometime. There is a difference between a Bible study course that, let's say, focuses on the Gospel of Matthew, and a down and dirty, here-it-is-in-Scripture sort of investigation of our theology. Dominic and I had been doing our best to learn as much as we could about Catholicism, but apologetics remained somewhat unfamiliar territory.

So, I put those journalistic skills to work again and started to research Catholic apologetics to find some answers. This opened up an entirely new world for me. I learned of a program called Catholic Answers and from then on started to fall in love, again, with the Eucharist, the Mass, the saints, Our Lady, and the entire Church. Nothing like a reformed Catholic to become an ardent fan of the Church! It was like I was back in Catholic grade school waiting eagerly to receive Jesus in Holy Communion for the very first time. I kept coming across names of Catholic apologists on various Catholic web sites; Dr. Scott Hahn, Jeff Cavins, Steve Ray, Rosalind Moss, and Al Kresta.

All of these apologists were amazing, but I was especially excited to see Al's name on the list. Al had left the Evangelical station a few years earlier after returning to the Catholic Church. He had just helped to launch a Catholic radio ministry, Ave Maria Radio, in Ann Arbor Michigan. I knew he was a top-rated talk show host, and also knew a little bit about his journey. I did not know, at that point in time, that he had such expertise in the area of apologetics, as well as Catholic evangelization. The more I learned about his ministry, and other similar efforts around the country, the more my desire to help re-evangelize Catholics grew. I was bumping into more and more Catholics who had left the Church but who had no idea what they actually left behind when they made that decision. So many had been impacted by the one-two punch of poor catechesis and culture influences that I could see how my media expertise and background in Protestant radio could be quite useful. The pieces of the puzzle of my life continued to be lovingly placed by the hand of God and the pace of events that occurred at that time still takes my breath away. And it hasn't slowed down since.

On Assignment:
A phrase applied to a journalist who is given a specific topic or issue to cover over a long term basis.

CHAPTER EIGHT
"On Assignment"

There is a big difference between reporters that are "on assignment" and those referred to as "general assignment" reporters. "On assignment" means you have been chosen, or set aside, to cover a specific story or news beat, as we say in the industry, in order to provide more in depth and continuous coverage. General assignment reporters walk into the newsroom every day, as I did for years, and are thrown into the mix of whatever happens to be breaking at the time. They are expected to gather their information (remember those five "w's" and the "h?"), write and deliver their story, and then move on to the next story.

When we are whom we are called to be, we will set the world ablaze.

Catherine of Siena

Both "general assignment" and "on assignment" reporting takes a great deal of hard work, dedication, and skill. However, it is a real gift as a journalist to be able to devote more time and effort to one issue or to cover one entity over a long period of time. The reporter spends time and energy increasing his or her knowledge about the subject matter; that knowledge is then shared with the audience through more comprehensive and thought-provoking stories. In retrospect, it was clear that my life as a journalist was moving from "general assignment" to "on assignment."

I was truly enjoying my time at the Evangelical radio station, and that definitely included all the apologetic challenges that were thrown my way. It was another important period of learning and growing. But after two and a half years of sitting behind the microphone of a Protestant station, I was starting to feel somewhat constrained. I desperately wanted to reach out to the Catholic audience and felt my hands were somewhat tied behind my back. And for an Italian American woman that wasn't a good thing if you get my drift!

Most listeners were Protestant and I completely understood that, from a programming sense, discussions on Catholicism needed to be somewhat limited. Although I still believe that the audience could have benefited from some regular basic catechesis about the Church to help in the area of ecumenism and dispel a lot of Catholic myths that are still so prevalent today. But that was not to be. It was time to, in a loving sense, "shake the dust from my feet," as it says in Matthew 10, and move forward. The change from general assignment to on assignment was underway because, as is often the case, the rumbling that started in my spirit had to be addressed. You know how that goes. That certain feeling of uncertainty in something that at one point had held you firmly in place suddenly seems less certain. So it was that my own career continued to evolve.

The nudges from the Holy Spirit were confirmed when I received a call from, and a subsequent job offer at, Ave Maria Radio. Dominic and I believed this was another great opportunity to learn and grow in our Catholic faith as well as a chance for me to use my media ministry to help Catholics engage the culture. I gratefully accepted the offer to host a radio program called "Catholic Connection." It went on the air in early December of 2002 as the network's local morning drive program.

In January 2006, a handful of years after our debut, Ave Maria Radio welcomed some late but great, "breaking news" from Birmingham, Alabama. Al Kresta's afternoon drive program "Kresta in the Afternoon," along with "Catholic Connection," had been picked up for national syndication through the EWTN Global Catholic Radio Network. As a result, our programs are now heard on over 120 stations around the country as well as Sirius Satellite Radio and the Internet. Meanwhile, thanks to the good Lord of course, as well as the support of my radio colleagues, my "misery has indeed become a ministry!"

What has happened to me can only have happened by the hand of God. There is simply no other explanation. Step by step, with each newsflash, God revealed more of His plan for me and in the process I grew to see, as well as respect, a different but much more exciting story that was developing for my life.

God of the beginning, God of the end, God of all creatures, Lord of all generations: with love You guide the world, with love You walk hand in hand with all the living.

Jewish meditation

It has been nearly six years since I took to the Catholic radio airwaves, and I have never felt happier or more fulfilled. Between the radio program and my work as a professional speaker, Catholic newspaper columnist, and author, I feel like a real "gal Friday." With the old-fashioned press credentials stuck in my hat, and pen and notebook in hand, I am "on assignment" for the Lord and His Church for as long as He sees fit. Interesting, isn't it?

I love the fact that the word Gospel actually means "Good **News**." When I was working in the secular end of **news** I was never truly happy for any length of time. I continued to experience that unsettling feeling of "I'm not there yet," not really knowing where "there" was and certainly not seeing that the journey itself was to become invaluable. The day to day accolades or successes of the secular media existence never fully satisfied me. I was always looking for more. As a result, I almost lost my marriage and my soul.

So, let me introduce you to my News Director and Executive Producer sitting in the Master Control room. His name is Jesus. And to recap the headlines for you, here is what He's done for me so far: He has healed my marriage, redeemed my life, and gave me a new career doing what I love -- reporting. Remember that little Catholic girl who eagerly went up to the microphone in the school gym to read her part in the Christmas production? She's still behind the microphone; only now she's come full circle.

What never ceases to amaze and humble me is the platform with which I have been entrusted. Ave Maria Radio, through EWTN syndication, not only reaches listeners across the country but around the world. The Eternal World Network is, after all, "global Catholic radio and TV." EWTN's executive producer, Doug Keck, as well as many others at the network, has been very supportive of my misery turned ministry goals. Most recently they have given me the honor of doing a mini-series, airing this fall, dedicated to media awareness and my first book, *Noise*. They have also given me opportunities to appear on several different EWTN flagship shows, including "Book Mark" with Doug Keck, "The Abundant Life" with Johnnette Benkovic, " The World Over" with Raymond Arroyo, "Faith and Culture" with Colleen Carroll Campbell, and "Life on the Rock" with Doug Barry and Fr. Mark. EWTN's Rome Bureau Chief Joan Lewis is a regular guest on my program joining me every Wednesday after the Papal audience. Joan has also become, as has Johnnette and others at EWTN, friends who continue to help me learn about the Catholic faith. Thom Price, John Pepe, and

Frank Leurck have welcomed me into the EWTN radio family and help make "Catholic Connection" the best it can be.

And to think that I believed the be-all and end-all was reporting the local news for one of my hometown stations. Who knew? We tend, in our limited humanity, to put God in a box. But it is incredibly important for us to always remember what Scripture teaches us:

Eye has not seen nor has ear heard what God has ready for those who love him (1 Corinthians 2:9).

Never in my wildest dreams could I ever imagine that I would be given the opportunity to use my gifts in such a mighty way for God. Or to get more to the heart of the matter, to realize that these gifts are God-given and as such are meant to be used for Him and His glory. "Catholic Connection" now regularly features many of the great Catholic men and women who helped form me in my faith; of course Al Kresta, but also Steve Ray, Jeff Cavins, and Rosalind Moss, who have also become good friends.

I heartily encourage you to consider the gifts the good Lord has given you and ask you to embrace the journey you've been on knowing that Jesus Christ is your Savior and friend. He is a confidant who is willing and able to do wonderful things for you and me when we keep our eyes on Him. Remember that His yoke is never burdensome nor requests impossible to fill. He has a plan for you, He has a plan for me, and together we can glorify His kingdom with our resounding "yes!"

If all this sounds exciting, stay tuned for, as Paul Harvey would say, "the rest of the story." Coming up next on this regularly scheduled newscast; the big scoop!

Scoop:
An informal news reporting term used to describe a major story of great significance, excitement, and especially surprise- a story that reveals previously unknown or secretative information.

CHAPTER NINE
"The Scoop"

The truth of the Church's teaching is proven in the wounds of those who reject it.

Christopher West, Theology of the Body Institute's Head and Heart
Immersion Course, June 2008

*T*hose words describe me, and what's happened in my life! I said to myself. It was another one of those "aha" newsflash moments. Those words were spoken just recently by well-known author and speaker Christopher West. It was June 2008, and Dominic and I were attending the powerful week-long "Head and Heart Immersion Course" offered by the Theology of the Body Institute in Pennsylvania.

Christopher West has been teaching, writing, and speaking internationally on John Paul II's Theology of the Body for many years. *"Theology of the Body"* refers to a series of 129 groundbreaking addresses presented by the late Holy Father early in his pontificate, from 1979 to 1984.

According to the Theology of the Body Institute, the talks provide *a profoundly beautiful vision of the human embodiment and erotic love.* John Paul II wanted the world to understand, as Christopher West would say, that "matter matters." Truly understanding our

Godly design, being made in God's image as male and female, leads to understanding the reason and meaning for our human existence; we are made to be a gift of self in relationship with our Creator, just as Christ gives Himself as the Bridegroom to the Church, the Bride.

Once we understand and accept that our anthropology is ordered by God and toward that relationship with Him, everything else falls into place. Without this we are left to our own assumptions, subject to outside cultural influences, which would have us believe that we exist only for "me, myself, and I."

In reality, we exist for a relationship with God. Anything less, and our bodies only matter in terms of our own needs, self interest, and gratification; this transforms us into a far inferior version of who God has called us to be. When we give in to our self interests we easily become "users" who "use" others as objects or a means of getting what we want.

I lived without the Church for so long that my life resembled a train wreck. That's why I couldn't write Christopher's quote down fast enough, and it took every ounce of strength to refrain myself from standing up and shouting, "Preach it, brother!" It was reminiscent of the overwhelming feeling I had experienced at the Rome Congress, a few short months prior, where we had examined John Paul II's letter on the dignity and vocation of women; "*Mulieris Dignitatem.*" Part of me wanted to remain in the auditorium. I remember distinctly feeling as if I were one of the women of Bethany, sitting at the feet of Christ, Himself.

Christopher West, as with the other presenters at the Vatican congress, provides conference goers with such meaningful insights. Drawing upon John Paul II's profound writings, these people help us delve deeper into the beauty, and Truth of Church teaching. I felt as if my heart would burst with gratitude and appreciation for the opportunities to study such profound material from some of the world's leading scholars and theologians.

But you are a "chosen race, a royal priesthood, a holy nation, a people of his own, so that you may announce the praises" of him who called you out of darkness into his wonderful light.

1 Peter 2:9

The other half of me felt as if I was being let in on the greatest secret; the secret to true happiness and fulfillment that had to be shared with the world. This wasn't some new-age pop culture book but the real power in the Truth of Christ. During both seminars I had the sudden urge to dash out, race toward the nearest microphone or megaphone, and excitedly announce "Newsflash!" or "Extra! Extra! Read all about it!" We have *the* scoop, the greatest story ever told; the story of the Gospel of Jesus Christ in the fullness of the Catholic faith. This must have been a small taste of apostolic experience at Pentecost. I was on fire for my Lord!

Think about this, again, for emphasis; the word Gospel actually means "Good News." When I was working in the secular end of plain old news, I was never truly happy, at least not for long. The recognition from fellow journalists was nice, as were the day-to-day accolades and successes, but nothing ever satisfied me. That's because nothing secular ever can fill that special place in our hearts made especially for God's indwelling.

Now I was truly fulfilled by doing something I never planned to do. I was still reporting the news but the story is the most important story I would ever cover in my life; the story of the Gospel and the saving work of Jesus Christ through the Catholic Church. One. Holy. Catholic. Apostolic. It simply cannot get more powerful than that.

This realization about the saving grace and Truth of the Catholic faith did not occur to me in a miraculous moment, although I have interviewed several people who have been blessed by such an experience. But for me, as you know by now, it started with a cry for help and then happened gradually over a long painful process which involved taking a good look at my life: past, present and what was missing.

It also took an honest reflection, and even investigation, on my own part. This process allowed me, Teresa Tomeo the reporter, along with me, Teresa Tomeo the woman, to see why the Catholic Church is indeed the "big scoop" that the world so desperately needs to hear. It is my prayer that if you are struggling with a particular tenet of the Catholic faith, or if you have a difficult time accepting certain Church teachings, that you will hang in there. Allow your heart to be transformed by your Creator. Ask God for the grace to open your heart and speak to you concerning your own walk with Him and to truly see how the areas the Church provides whatever it is that you need. Have an open and honest discussion with God and share with Him things that may trouble or bother you, even if they are occurring in the Church. Keep nothing from Him; not your joy nor your sorrow.

I have found that most people leave the Church because they don't truly know what she teaches. Additionally, many people think the Church dogmas are unrealistic, outdated, and too difficult to apply to their lives when, in actuality, Church teachings, or more precisely, God's teachings, are meant for our well-being. God's plan is always the best plan. We only need to ask for His help in applying it in our daily lives.

Others may have been wounded by poor catechesis or hurt by a priest or lay religious leader who may have acted uncharitably or in an unforgiving manner. Many Catholics have also been affected by scandals that have occurred, especially in recent years. Please remember, though, that the Church continues to confront these issues. Just as we grow from our own faults and challenges, so to is our precious Church growing from some of the faults and challenges with some of those who are assigned to do her work.

During his April 2008 visit to the United States, Pope Benedict XVI not only met privately with victims of the priest abuse scandal but addressed the scandal directly and very publicly on several different occasions. This was a key part of his April 16th message to the United States Conference of Catholic Bishops as he referred to the abuse of minors by priests among the "countersigns to the Gospel of life found in America" that still causes deep shame.

Many of you have spoken to me of the enormous pain that your communities have suffered when clerics have betrayed their priestly obligations and duties by such gravely immoral behavior. As you strive to eliminate this evil wherever it occurs, you may be assured of the prayerful support of God's people throughout the world. Rightly, you attach priority to showing compassion and care to the victims. It is your God-given responsibility as pastors to bind up the wounds caused by every breach of trust, to foster healing, to promote reconciliation and to reach out with loving concern to those so seriously wronged.

Responding to this situation has not been easy and, as the President of your Episcopal Conference has indicated, it was 'sometimes very badly handled.' Now that the scale and gravity of the problem is more clearly understood, you have been able to adopt more focused remedial and disciplinary measures and to promote a safe environment that gives greater protection to young people. While it must be remembered that the overwhelming majority of clergy and religious in America do outstanding work in bringing the liberating message of the Gospel to the people entrusted to their care, it is vitally important that the vulnerable always be shielded from those who would cause harm. In this regard, your efforts to heal and protect are bearing great fruit not only for those directly under your pastoral care, but for all of society.

Women's issues represent another major stumbling block. Many hold the view that the Church has done little to advance the causes of women or have held women back. But how many are aware of how sincerely John Paul II apologized for whatever role the Church may have played in the mistreatment of women over the centuries?

In his 1995 Letter to Women, John Paul II openly apologized to women around the world for any hurt caused to them by those in the Church. The letter was written to women on the eve of the Fourth World Conference on Women held in Beijing. In the letter, the Pope acknowledged that we are "unfortunately heirs to a history that has conditioned us" and that the "conditioning" has been an obstacle to the progress of women.

Women's dignity has often been unacknowledged and their prerogatives misrepresented; they have often been relegated to the margins of society and even reduced to servitude. This has prevented women from truly being themselves and it has resulted in a spiritual impoverishment of humanity. Certainly it is no easy task to assign the blame for this, considering the many kinds of cultural conditioning which down the centuries have shaped ways of thinking and acting. And if objective blame, especially in particular historical contexts, has belonged to not just a few members of the Church, for this I am truly sorry. May this regret be transformed, on the part of the whole Church, into a renewed commitment of fidelity to the Gospel vision. When it comes to setting women free from every kind of exploitation and domination, the Gospel contains an ever relevant message which goes back to the attitude of Jesus Christ himself. Transcending the established norms of his own culture, Jesus treated women with openness, respect, acceptance and tenderness. In this way he honored the dignity which women have always possessed according to God's plan and in his love. As we look to Christ at the end of this Second Millennium, it is natural to ask ourselves: how much of his message has been heard and acted upon?

John Paul II went even further, pointing out the oppression, discrimination, and exploitation of women that is so contrary to the Gospel of Jesus Christ. He referred to many of the problems facing women today such as benefits for working mothers, equal work for equal pay, and equality in job advancement. John Paul II was a visionary and a blessing to our Church. His papal writings are a treasure that continues to reveal the love and Truth that is found in Christ.

And what shall we say of the obstacles which in so many parts of the world still keep women from being fully integrated into social, political and economic life? We need only think of how the gift of motherhood is often penalized rather than rewarded, even though humanity owes its very survival to this gift. Certainly, much remains to be done to prevent discrimination against those who have chosen to be wives and mothers. As far as personal rights are concerned, there is an urgent need to achieve real equality in every area: equal pay for equal work, protection for working mothers, fairness in career advancements, equality of spouses with regard to family rights and the recognition of everything that is part of the rights and duties of citizens in a democratic state.

I haven't done a survey, so I don't have any official numbers, but in my work as a Catholic talk show host and speaker, it is my experience that only a handful of the millions of Catholics in this country, not to mention the more than one billion Catholics around the world, are familiar with these honest and humble words from two of our popes. Nor have most Catholics been properly introduced to the countless documents, letters, and papal encyclicals that directly address sensitive, personal, and very real human issues with which the average Catholic struggles. Too often, and again I am speaking from experience here, we form our opinions about Church doctrine from what we see or hear in the mass media. Big mistake. Fatal error.

One particularly sensitive area in today's culture, which has been dominated by radical feminist ideology, relates to male priesthood in the Catholic Church. We are led to believe if we listen to the voices in the culture, that the Catholic Church is denying women the "right" to advance in the Church. The Church is often mistakenly viewed as another company or industry that is holding women back professionally in some way, shape, or form. But the Church, as I just pointed out, is the Bride of Christ. The priest is "In Persona Christi," representing the Bridegroom, Christ. Simply put, a bride can't marry a bride. This goes against the natural design of the marital union, which represents the union of Christ and His Church. Just as men are not able to bear children, a woman cannot be ordained a priest. The priesthood is also not a "right," it is a calling and a vocation.

In the passage from *Mulieris Dignitatem,* John Paul II explains how this is part of the great mystery given to us in the Eucharist.

We find ourselves at the very heart of the Paschal Mystery, which completely reveals the spousal love of God. Christ is the Bridegroom because "he has given himself": his body has been "given", his blood has been "poured out" (cf. Lk 22:19-20). In this way "he loved them to the end" (Jn 13:1). The "sincere gift" contained in the Sacrifice of the Cross gives definitive prominence to the spousal meaning of God's love. As the Redeemer of the world, Christ is the Bridegroom of the Church. The Eucharist is the Sacrament of our Redemption. It is the Sacrament of the Bridegroom and of the Bride. The Eucharist makes present and realizes anew in a sacramental manner the redemptive act of Christ, who "creates" the Church, his body. Christ is united with this "body" as the bridegroom with the bride. All this is contained in the Letter to the Ephesians. The perennial "unity of the two" that exists between man and woman from the very "beginning" is introduced into this "great mystery" of Christ and of the Church.

Since Christ, in instituting the Eucharist, linked it in such an explicit way to the priestly service of the Apostles, it is legitimate to conclude that he thereby wished to express the relationship between man and woman, between what is "feminine" and what is "masculine". It is a relationship willed by God both in the mystery of creation and in the mystery of Redemption. It is the Eucharist above all that expresses the redemptive act of Christ the Bridegroom towards the Church the Bride. This is clear and unambiguous when the sacramental ministry of the Eucharist, in which the priest acts "in persona Christi", is performed by a man (MD 26).

I worked in the secular media so I am guilty on two fronts; first in buying into what the media was selling me and secondly, and maybe more egregiously, for regurgitating the lies that were being perpetrated by an industry that was plagued with an anti-Catholic and generally ant-Christian bias. I publicly admit my shame in that I did not take the time nor have the interest to research and then report on a number of topics, especially pertaining to the Catholic Church teaching, accurately or fairly.

I think there are countless Catholics, particularly women, who, if aware of their true worth to the Church, would come running back with open arms and fling themselves at the foot of the Cross. I know I did, and that is why I take my new assignment so seriously. I am also here to proclaim from the rooftops that as surely as you may open your arms to Christ, He has already opened His arms to you. You ARE forgiven for your past and should embrace that forgiveness. Do not believe lies that you can't be forgiven or that you've done something too big for God's mercy. That is spiritual warfare at work. You are a soul worth fighting for and I am asking you to acknowledge the reality that Christ has already fought the good fight and won. Don't let road blocks keep you from coming back home. God loves you and wants you to tap into all gifts He has for you; most especially in the Sacraments of the Church. If I can come back, be forgiven, and embrace the Catholic Church, anyone can. God loves you and wants you back in relationship with Him, regardless of what you have done.

> *I gave in, and admitted that God was God.*
>
> C. S. Lewis

Truth is indeed proven through the wounds of those who reject it. I know this on a personal and professional level. My own wounds proved to be a groundswell of Truth. Then, working in the media, I have conducted research on the massive amount of evidence proving the extent of our wounds as a culture. These wounds, ultimately, are proving out the Truth of the Church teachings. For instance, the Church has always taught about the sanctity of life, family, and the dignity of the person. These aren't new teachings for the Church but centuries old. Now, studies prove out what the Church has always taught; that there will be true societal problems without the family (one man and one woman) as the epicenter. Indeed, in recent years Church teaching has been affirmed, and reaffirmed, over and over again by countless studies showing the fallout from divorce, abortion, sexual promiscuity, birth control, embryonic stem cell research, and euthanasia. Ironically, most of the research in these areas is being done by secular think tanks, organizations, and public universities. The same machines that put time and energy into bringing down the Church provide information that builds up the Church.

Looking at the problematic patterns in my own life, I can see that from the time I was a child I bought into the "me" agenda. I aggressively pushed forward with my own selfish interests, leaving God in the dust. Feelings, in terms of what I wanted or needed, became the arbiter for everything in my life and led to a great deal of sin. To put it in Theology of the Body terminology, matter mattered -- but for selfish reasons and goals. Most of us have fallen prey to this at one time or another, but it is only through those extreme close-ups that we are able to truly see and make a conscious choice to change. God, I have found, is always mercifully giving us opportunities!

By my late teen years my ideas about morality and sexuality soon started to echo the moral relativism of society that is even more prevalent today; if it feels good, do it. I'm pretty sure there were bumper stickers and posters perpetuating this attitude. Abortion and contraception, for example, were just means to an end, with the end being the person's own desires. While I never had an abortion, for a long time, God forgive me, I gave it little or no thought and when it came up in conversation I took the typical lukewarm, safe approach; "I would never have one but who am I to tell some other woman what she can or can't do with her body."

I distinctly remember one of these times. Dominic and I were newlyweds and once-in-a-blue-moon would visit a beautiful parish located down the street from our first apartment on Detroit's east side. Ironically this parish is the home to many beautiful events that I frequently feature on "Catholic Connection." It always was, and still is, a wonderfully orthodox parish with priests that are not shy about preaching the Truth in love, especially when it comes to the life issues. On this particular Sunday, the priest was giving a strong homily regarding abortion. I refused to listen and immediately started shifting in my seat, getting angrier by the minute. I blocked out His comments with my hardened heart. When we left Mass I told Dom that I thought the priest was way out of line. However, I had never read any of the Church teachings on this issue nor discussed it with any religious or lay leaders. I was woefully ignorant on this issue, as well as on the contraception issue.

He bestows on them beauty instead of ashes, the oil of gladness instead of mourning and a garment of praise instead of a spirit of despair.

Isaiah 61:3

How arrogant to be able to come to so many forgone conclusions about such serious issues without doing any homework or soul searching. I had always prided myself on my "intellect" and my ability to research and study various topics. Doing your homework, or answering the five "w's" and the "h," remember, was a catch phrase for journalists which referred to a reporter's efforts to find out as much about a subject matter as possible before conducting an interview or filing a story. Interesting how I could sniff out all the pertinent details I needed when it suited me, but abstain when it came to controversial topics that, in retrospect, clearly made me squirm deep down inside; where God was still connected to me. That Sunday homily was a perfect example of the way in which most of us aren't open to the whole Truth of the Church but also, sadly, the way in which we have bought into the secular message that we shouldn't be responsible to anyone or anything other than ourselves. God did not intend for us to act selfishly and without regard but, rather, with the greater good as our goal.

I formed my own opinions based on my own "feelings" along with information I had heard, out there "in the world," that was often tainted. Add to that what I chose to believe and I had a sort of a religious "smoothie." A little of this, a little of that, and I was good to go. Sadly, on the abortion issue, my smoothie allowed me to convince myself that it wasn't the child but the "choice" that was more important.

Now that I have availed myself of the Church teachings, particularly the *Catechism,* I am deeply saddened by the realization that abortion is both the taking of a life and is also, by nature, evil. Had I bothered to look a little more closely at even the secular research, I might have changed my mind on this issue realizing that my "intellect" had been duped, or sold a huge bill of goods, from Planned Parenthood, the National Organization for Women, and other pro-abortion groups who make abortion sound like something as easy as getting your teeth cleaned or your eyes checked. I had no idea the impact abortion had on women, men, and society in general. Statistics are mind boggling:

- More than four thousand abortions occur every day in the United States alone.
- 40%-60% of women who have abortions report negative reactions.
- More than half of women who have abortions felt forced or pressured to have an abortion.

- One abortion doubles a woman's risk of breast cancer.
- One abortion increases risks of other cancers in women including ovarian, liver, and cervical cancer.
- Abortion is connected to increase risks of drug abuse, alcohol abuse, and eating disorders in women.
- Three out of four men report difficulty with an abortion experience.
- Men connected to abortion are likely to also experience depression, anxiety, pornography addictions, and relational problems.

So much for "safe, legal, and rare," as they say!

As I started to come back to the Church I knew I had to get right with God on a number of issues in my life. Abortion was one of them. So was the big "C" or the contraception issue that no one wants to talk about. That's *the* problem. Contraception is still the white elephant in the living room that everyone likes to pretend isn't there even though this, too, is sited as intrinsically evil in the *Catechism.*

Saints are sinners who kept on going.

Robert Louis Stevenson

My husband and I were not given any information warning us from artificial contraception, or encouraging us to consider natural family planning (NFP) when we were married 25 years ago in the Catholic Church. Then again, we didn't ask about it, either. So while some of the culpability lies with those running the marriage prep program, we were also culpable. Both of us knew vaguely that contraception was against Church teaching but we never bothered to look into it to any real degree. Again, as with the abortion issue, I never sought the wisdom of, or behind, Church teachings.

Here, as with abortion, a little fact checking on my part would have uncovered the myriad problems with contraception. Contraception tragically barricades the working of God in marriage. It is physical, spiritual, and emotional. In all ways it is the violation of our relationship with God. Contraception is saying that you are not completely open to giving and receiving in the marital act and are instead using the marital act for sexual gratification rather than a mutual exchange of total self giving love. The person and the act become an object. Although I didn't realize it at the time, contraception added to our marriage problems as Dom and I were not totally open to one another as husband and wife.

However, as many people know, even when a marriage is in conformance to God's ultimate plan to be fruitful and multiply, a couple does not always conceive. For us, remaining childless was neither a purposeful nor conscious decision. As we worked on our marriage and began to fully embrace Church teachings, we found that our lives had evolved in a way that would not include our own biological children. Instead, we became spiritual parents to people who have come into our lives and also to our ministries. Paramount to understanding what it means to be a "spiritual parent" has been John Paul II's teaching, in *"Mulieris Dignitatem,"* where he emphatically states that all women are giving "birth" in one sense or another. For me, as in all things, I can look back and see with clarity how God has used me for His purpose. Indeed, I feel that this has been how Dom and I were called to respond to the Lord.

But let's get back to my interest in shedding light on Church teachings in regards to contraception and abortion. As I tried to point out through earlier examples, Church teaching is always affirmed through subjective experience. Or, as Christopher West says, *"Truth is indeed proven through the wounds of those who reject it."* Contraception has been packaged and cloaked in words like "choice" and "freedom." Find me anyone alive who doesn't respond to the emotion of those words!

With contraception, just as with abortion, society has been subjected to the agendas of many organizations wishing to promote the culture of death. We've been "had," big time. This is sadly but especially true of women. We wrongfully assumed freedom was tied to things that actually bound us; while the things we avoided because we felt they bound us, truly set us free!

Our culture, in many ways thanks to the sexual revolution and the push from radical feminism, has come to believe that abortion and contraception are "rights" that equal "freedom." Tragically, these evils have led to women being even more abused, objectified, exploited, and degraded; injustices the radical feminist complained so strongly about and fought so hard against are the same injustices Pope Paul VI warned, in *Humanae Vitae,* would occur in monumental proportions if the contraceptive mentality was allowed to continue.

> *Let them first consider how easily this course of action could open wide the way for marital infidelity and a general lowering of moral standards. Not much experience is needed to be fully aware of human weakness and to understand that human beings—and especially the young, who are so exposed to temptation—need incentives to keep the moral law, and it is an evil thing to make it easy for them to break that law. Another effect that gives cause for alarm is that a man who grows accustomed to the use of contraceptive methods may forget the reverence due to a woman, and, disregarding her physical and emotional equilibrium, reduce her to being a mere instrument for the satisfaction of his own desires, no longer considering her as his partner whom he should surround with care and affection.*

Prophetic indeed! In February 2007, the American Psychological Association came out with an alarming report showing how the "sexualization of girls" leads to a host of problems including increased risks of developing eating disorders, depression, and low self-esteem.

What does "sexualization" mean? Ironically (or maybe not so ironically, and I doubt that the APA would see the connection), the problem is caused by exactly what was outlined by Pope Paul VI more than forty years ago: the objectification of women.

I find it chilling that an entire generation of young girls has been preyed upon by organizations proclaiming to act in their best interests. These girls have become victims of objectification in its most vile forms: pornography, prostitution, and the abject attitude that comes from the emotional issues that are inherently attached to such degradation. The APA cited several major components to sexualization saying it occurs when:

- A person's value comes only from her or his sexual appeal or behavior.
- A person is held to a standard that equates physical attractiveness with being sexy.
- A person is sexually objectified-that is, made into a thing for others' sexual use.
- Sexuality is inappropriately imposed upon a person.

All we have to do is, again, turn on the computer or the television, pick up a magazine, or walk into a mall to see how women are repeatedly being objectified. Can it be that simple? To a degree, yes. Each of us knows, all too intimately, the pull of the secular world. If a human is, by nature, fragile; then the onslaught of messages that literally fill the airwaves can only push the fragile human in a negative direction or situation.

Pornography is a 10-to-20 billion dollar a year industry. There are now over 4 million pornographic web sites on the World Wide Web. But that's not all, folks. There's so much more to back up the wisdom of Church teaching, which places human dignity and the right to life above all else.

Artificial contraception is not as safe as you may have been led to believe, another example of the massive cultural misinformation campaign that's been promoted through the media for decades. A tremendous amount of research exists on the dangers of artificial birth control. Understanding the benefits and beauty of what the Church teaches on natural family planning is a gift that you and your family will cherish.

The knowledge of natural family planning is a gift to give your friends, your grown children, your newly married children, and your extended family members. Once again, the Church shares a sincere understanding of what Christ taught in regards to this matter,

For the Mighty One has done great things for me and holy is his name.

Luke 1:49

and is vindicated by the same institutions that wish to bring it down. There is research on the hazards of the birth control pill, which has been shown to increase risks of breast cancer, ovarian cancer, heart disease, hypertension and a number of other medical problems. Many forms of birth control are also abortifacients, drugs that can cause abortions.

So here we are, living in a world that tells us consistently through all media possible, that we should all be able to do whatever we want and with whomever we want as long as we are happy and feel good. But I didn't feel good when I was buying in to this lie and according to the research, that's pretty much the case with a lot of other folks too, especially my sweet sisters-in-Christ. Have we really "come a long way, Baby," as the old Virginia Slims cigarette commercial used to proclaim? I don't think so.

We need to be honest with the Lord and with ourselves. We are being called to look deep within and see who or what we are allowing to form our conscience. More pointedly, we may even need to ask ourselves if our conscience has even been formed at all. Too many of us have been reactive instead of pro-active. We get caught up in the tides of change and then look back and wonder if the change has been worth it, knowing that it has not. Unfortunately, we don't always think on our own but allow our thoughts and ideas to be spoon fed to us through the media saturated culture which tells us that putting yourself first is what counts.

A well-formed conscience, however, does not mean reading a few articles or watching a few newscasts and then saying, "Well, I think or feel this (or that) way." According to the *Catechism,* we form our conscience through the guidance of the Holy Spirit and the teachings of the Church:

> *In the formation of conscience the Word of God is the light for our path, we must assimilate it in faith and prayer and put it into practice. We must also examine our conscience before the Lord's Cross. We are assisted by the Holy Spirit, aided by the witness or the advice of others, and guided by the authoritative teachings of the Church.*

This is why so much evil has become so acceptable. Morality has been left up to the individual; I'm okay, you're okay. If you believe one thing, that's fine; if I believe something else, that's fine too. It is the "PC" approach that has become so prevalent. We don't want to offend anyone, so we "tolerate" just about everything. Although I don't know who said it first, a great quote that is worth sharing: If you are too open-minded, your brains will fall out. To a culture that prides itself on being "open-minded," these are excellent, cautionary words.

Pope Benedict XVI has made this idea of relativism a theme of his pontificate. During his address to the members of the International Theological Commission in October of 2007, the Holy Father pointed to the importance of seeking guidance from the ultimate Source, Almighty God, and spoke of the "inalienable value of the natural moral law." Without this, the Holy Father warned, the very foundation of democratic order was susceptible to erosion and destruction:

> *Today, a positivist conception of law seems to dominate many thinkers. They claim that humanity or society or indeed the majority of citizens is becoming the ultimate source of civil law. The problem that arises is not; therefore, the search for good but the search for powers, or rather, how to balance powers.*

> *At the root of this trend is ethical relativism, which some even see as one of the principal conditions for democracy, since relativism is supposed to guarantee tolerance of and reciprocal respect for people. But if this were so, the majority of a moment would become the ultimate source of law.*

> *History very clearly shows that most people can err. True rationality is not guaranteed by the consensus of a large number but solely by the transparency of human reason to creative Reason and by listening together to this Source of our rationality.*

When the fundamental requirements of human dignity, of human life, of the family institution, of a fair social order, in other words, basic human rights, are at stake, no law devised by human beings can subvert the law that the Creator has engraved on the human heart without the indispensable foundations of society itself being dramatically affected.

Natural law thus becomes the true guarantee offered to each one in order that he may live in freedom, have his dignity respected and be protected from all ideological manipulation and every kind of arbitrary use or abuse by the stronger.

No one can ignore this appeal. If, by tragically blotting out the collective conscience, skepticism and ethical relativism were to succeed in deleting the fundamental principles of the natural moral law, the foundations of the democratic order itself would be radically damaged.

To prevent this obscuring, which is a crisis of human civilization even before it is a Christian one, all consciences of people of good will, of lay persons and also of the members of the different Christian denominations, must be mobilized so that they may engage, together and effectively, in order to create the necessary conditions for the inalienable value of the natural moral law in culture and in civil and political society to be fully understood.

Indeed, on respect for this natural moral law depends the advance of individuals and society on the path of authentic progress in conformity with right reason, which is participation in the eternal Reason of God.

I kidded myself for years that I had all the right reasons when it came to abortion and contraception. I was proud of being politically correct. Abortion and contraception were "private" decisions that affected only the person who made them, or so I continually tried to convince myself. But as John Paul II often said, "sin is never singular." The so-called "personal choice" of abortion has cost this country the lives of nearly 50 million unborn babies and deeply hurt millions of men and women. Yes, the scales were falling off my eyes.

It is my prayer that if this book leads one person to the resources (offered in the back section of the book) for such things as post-abortive healing, I will have gladly spent my time in writing. The contraceptive mentality of this country has caused countless abortions and led to a horrible degradation and objectification of women. Statistics can probably never relate the overall impact and breakdown of relationships due to these causal factors.

Once I started to examine the evidence, and more importantly my conscience, I knew I had to head straight to the confessional, open my heart to the Truth of Church teaching, and change many of my own immoral practices. It clearly had to begin with me. But that was only the first step in a series of steps that would become increasingly easier to take. Steps that at times could even be seen as skipping because my heart was so filled with love for Christ. I was embracing my journey more than ever before.

That next big step, then, was a giant one; I had to tell the world what I knew. Things were moving from private acceptance to public proclamations. I had to break the big scoop, the real story about true "freedom" found through embracing all of the teachings of the one, holy, Catholic, and apostolic faith.

So do not be afraid of them. There is nothing concealed that will not be disclosed, or hidden that will not be made known. What I tell you in the dark, speak in the daylight; what is whispered in your ear, proclaim from the rooftops (Matthew 10:26-28).

Development Programme

Ballistic

The Rebel Son

ome fill prescriptions on the black

arket: oth

the Fee

the One

True Faith

or High St

Bottom of the Deck

idden

Election-Day Forecast
around the world!

Out but Not Do

Developing Story:
A story of major significance updated by
media outlets on a regular basis with
important information or "developments."

CHAPTER TEN
"Developing Story"

When a reporter works on a major developing story, it means he or she is expected to file updates on a regular basis. The story is assigned to one particular reporter whose responsibility it becomes to concentrate on building sources and compiling additional, important facts that will help keep the audience or reader informed.

It's a lot like our own daily lives, isn't it? We are all assigned a major developing story at baptism. And by virtue of that sacrament we are called to tell that story, to evangelize. Hopefully the updates we file will include new and exciting information we've learned from our daily walk with God. The reports we give to our family and friends, as we continue to write this developing story, will affirm and encourage those we come in contact with; just as the developing story on the evening news, or in the morning paper, are designed to do that as well.

Now to him who is able to accomplish far more than all we ask or imagine, by the power at work within us, to him be glory in the church and in Christ Jesus to all generations, forever and ever. Amen.

Ephesians 3:20-21

A good reporter has solid instincts or a "nose for news." He or she knows when to follow up on a solid lead and when to toss aside frivolous details that might confuse the audience or reader. A reporter who is able to deliver the "big scoop" doesn't allow erroneous information or inconsequential details to divert attention away from the main issue. A journalist cares about (or ought to care about) his or her reputation, and thus has an interest in not disseminating false information to the public. There is an old but very important saying in the news business: "consider the source." That's why the best reporters use reliable sources that can be trusted to provide the latest accurate information. Without good sources and good instincts, a reporter is at the mercy of anyone who might be looking for revenge, fifteen minutes of fame, or has an ax to grind.

In the development of our spiritual life, or our personal story with God, our conscience and the voice of the Holy Spirit represent that "nose for news." They combine to give us that journalistic instinct. Looking back on my own developing story I hope you can now see how those instincts were stifled or drowned out by some fairly disreputable sources. I followed far too many false leads and took one too many cues from the culture. As a result, the story I told with my life, for a while, was bad news.

Today I encourage you to consider ways in which your "nose for news" has been a valuable tool and express gratitude for your own conscience and the Holy Spirit's guidance. On the other hand, if you've found that you are not as pleased with the way your life is progressing as you would like, stop and think about how you are building that developing story, because it is in development. Ask yourself some tough questions that will allow you to get to the bottom of your story. Who or what is your source? Where is your information coming from, and do you really have the facts? Are you open to the Holy Spirit? Or are those journalistic instincts numbed by the pull of the world? Are you carefully compiling good information and sorting through the facts or merely rushing through while trying to meet that story deadline?

As Christians we sometimes believe we are "all that and a bag of chips," as one of my friends would say. You know, we have the Lord, so we definitely have our act together right? Well, grab your Bible and starting reading, especially the New Testament. The Apostles had the Lord physically right in front of them, miracles and all, but boy did they have some issues! And my friends, so do we.

Case in point is a major survey released in July 2007. Data gathered from 20 thousand Christians ranging in age from 15 to 88, and spanning 139 countries, showed that six out 10 of all the believers surveyed admitted the "busy-ness" of life kept them from God. These were not atheists or agnostics who were questioned but Christians; Christians around the globe running from task to task. In a July 30, 2007 on-line interview with "The Christian Post," researcher Dr. Michael Zigarelli, associate professor with Charleston Southern University, called it tragic.

> *The very people who could best help us escape the bondage of busyness are themselves in chains…. The accelerated pace and the activity level of the modern day distracts us from God and separates us from the abundant joyful, victorious life he desires for us.*

Dr. Zigarelli, who conducted the study, also told The Christian Post that the problem was prompted by what he termed "cultural conformity." If we are taking our cues on our schedules from the culture, suffice it to say it's not a huge leap that we are also being influenced by the world in a lot of other ways. In the last chapter I discussed the importance of a well-formed conscience. The *Catechism* explains that forming our conscience happens through meditating on the Scriptures, reading and studying the teachings of the Catholic Church, and seeking the guidance of the Holy Spirit. When we are actively involved in the process, and thus forming our conscience on the right things, we are able to seek guidance and make the proper decisions in our lives.

Fallacies do not cease to be fallacies because they become fashions.

G.K. Chesterton

This is especially true in the area of faith and morals, which are, in essence, the whole of our lives. No matter who we are or what vocation we desire or have, we fill it as Catholics first. So, I am a Catholic wife, journalist, talk show host, and author. You may be a Catholic lawyer and mother while someone else may be a Catholic teacher and grandmother. You see where I'm headed with this? No matter what, we cannot remove ourselves from who we are as Catholics and everything else follows. Thus, the only conclusion is that the formation of our conscience, actively and with enthusiasm, must be a top priority in our lives. Otherwise, we cannot fully be what God has called us to be to ourselves, to one another, or to Him. This means we cannot be too busy for God!

While one survey reports that Christians are too busy for God, there are hundreds of other surveys and reports that show people, in general, are lulled into believing just about anything and everything they read, watch, or listen to in the mass media and entertainment industry. This is based upon the vast amount of research that I did on my first book and the research that I continue to stay aware of in my role as media evangelist. According to the Parents TV Council, violence on TV has increased dramatically over the last few years. By the time your child or grandchild reaches 13 years old, he or she will have witnessed over 100,000 violent acts on TV alone and that number doubles to 200,000 by the time he or she graduates from high school. The facts concerning sexual content aren't any better. Soap operas are 24 times as likely to show sexual activity between unmarried couples while children view an average 14,000 sexual messages a year on television alone. Is it any wonder that one in four sexually active teen girls has contracted a sexually transmitted disease, according to the Centers for Disease Control, or that teen pregnancy is on the rise again?

Scary, isn't it? Despite all that we know about media influence, too many people are still forming opinions about crucial matters dealing with faith and morals from what they see on television or read in the newspaper. This doesn't mean that we should all grab our TV sets and throw them out the window. That's not what I am saying or what the Church says. But the Church does say we must be smart media consumers and that we must also engage the culture by questioning what's thrown at us 24/7, instead of just taking it, no pun intended, as Gospel.

> *Then He said to his disciples, "The harvest is plentiful but the workers are few."*
>
> Matthew 9:37

Every good reporter also has solid reference books at their fingertips, information they check daily to keep them at the top of their game. How about you? I am sure you own a Bible, but do you read from God's word daily? Do you own a daily Catholic devotional that can help you grow in your knowledge of Scripture? Do you have the *Catechism of the Catholic Church* and refer to it often? And are you visiting with *the* Source on a regular basis? Is Mass, as well as confession, a regular part of your life? Are you watching wholesome programming that uplifts your Christian values? Are you spending too much time with the media outlets in your home and less with God and family? Just a few questions to jot down as you continue on your assignment.

It could be that we are influenced by some other negative sources, such as guilt or discouragement, telling us we are not good enough or strong enough to step out in faith and make a difference. If these sources are causing you a severe case of writer's block, well, now is the time to scratch them right out of your reporter's notebook and start making a new list of contacts. How about scheduling some one-on-one interviews with members of the Communion of Saints?

As Catholics we have such a great cloud of witnesses who have gone before us leaving behind some of the most exhilarating stories ever written or told for Christ. Unfortunately, too few of us tap into their greatness as often as we should. Our saints will motivate, inspire, and uplift you every day as you do your best to develop an award winning story for Jesus.

Remember we are in the world, not of the world, as Scripture tells us, so life is going to throw a lot of static and interference our way. This is a ***developing*** story. I can't stress that enough. It's not "off the tower," yet, as we say in broadcasting. Don't give up. It is still unfolding. Pay attention to those newsflashes and make sure *the* director is still calling the shots from Master Control and can be heard loudly and clearly through that IFB.

Indeed, we are all works in progress. As you have seen up-close and personal with the story of my life, things will change from time to time, and every once in a while some of what we think is the best material, will end up on the editing room floor. That's okay. Remember how all the challenges and painful moments in my own life ending up also being blessings in disguise? Somehow, even though I did not recognize it at the time, they were used for God's glory. Whether it was my disappointment in the changes occurring in the news business, the challenges in my marriage, or the challenges from former Catholics about the Church, eventually I learned how to use them to make a difference. Consider ways in which your own disappointments may be working for your own growth and for the glory of God's kingdom.

Think back to the beginning of my story, "my extreme close–up" on the unemployment line. That was one of the most humbling experiences in my life – and yet, that experience now enables me to write and speak about facing change and re-inventing one's self in accordance to Church teachings. That was also the beginning of my journey back to Jesus and the Church. Marital troubles that eventually found healing through our time, effort, and commitment by the gift of God's mercy and graces, propelled my husband and me to share our testimony at marriage enrichment seminars and conferences. The attacks on the Church from former Catholics turned me into a mini-apologist. Finally, my frustrations with the media gave me a brand new ministry as a speaker and evangelist. Remember those fateful words I heard that settled into my heart? *Let your misery be your ministry.*

The road to success is dotted with many tempting parking places.

Author Unknown

Ask God what He wants you to learn from the suffering you may be experiencing. Learn from your mistakes, but don't look back at the "if's, shoulda coulda or woulda's" and think that you were happier or safer in your old environment. Be honest and consider where you came from and why moving forward, despite the pruning that no doubt will occur, is crucial to you being the best you can be for Christ.

If you are in the desert, spend time contemplating the beauty of the Exodus story in Scripture. Ponder the journey of the Israelites. See how your journey may be similar. Remember that freedom from slavery was all God's people could think and talk about but they also had to play a role in that freedom. Moses, at first, was their hero. Didn't it feel good to walk away from Pharaoh and on toward the Promised Land? Well, everything was great until they started wandering in the desert. It was too hot or too cold. The food just wasn't good enough. They missed the meat and vegetables they had while in captivity.

Even when they were given manna -- bread from heaven, directly from God -- they complained. The weather wasn't all that great, and they insisted that going back to Egypt would be better than the troubles they were encountering on their way to the land of milk and honey. It seems that it might be easier to be like the Israelites of the desert and clamor to go back to our old lives. We may want to buy into the adage "the devil that we know is better than the devil we don't know." Change is scary. But deep down, if we've come this far we know we have to go on. Christian singer and songwriter Sarah Groves talks about this in a beautiful song, "Painting Pictures of Egypt:"

> *I've been painting pictures of Egypt, leaving out what it lacked. The future looks so hard and I want to go back. But the places that used to fit me cannot hold the things I have learned and those roads were closed off to me while my back was turned.*

When I think what a mistake it would have been if I had followed my earlier inclinations towards the secular and away from my faith, I am chilled to the bone. I don't want to think about what I would have missed if I had decided to give up on my marriage or stay in the news business.

St. Teresa of Avila, the great mystic and doctor of the Church, who also happens to be my very favorite saint, reminds us how often our fear results in us putting God in a box.

> *We are tempted to stay mired in our failures, to limit our lives to what we can imagine, to the security of what we are comfortable with. Left to ourselves we strike a bargain with our faults and failings, believing them to be our destiny. But there is within our limitations, our faults and failures, a divinely conceived creature waiting to be released, waiting to break through to a level of life only God can conceive.*

This life is God's precious gift to you. And as Eleanor Powell said, "What you do with this life, and what you become, is your gift to God." Pope Benedict asked some profound questions of the young people attending the closing Mass at 2008 World Youth Day in Sydney, Australia. Questions that all Christians should ask themselves:

> *Dear young people, let me now ask you a question. What will you leave to the next generation? Are you building your lives on firm foundations, building something that will endure? Are you living your lives in a way that opens up space for the Spirit in the midst of a world that wants to forget God, or even rejects him in the name of a falsely conceived freedom? How are you using the gifts you have been given, the 'power' which the Holy Spirit is even now prepared to release within you?"*

Please allow me to give you, from the depths of my heart, a few more beautiful words of Teresa of Avila:

> *And so the feeling remains, that God is on the journey too.*

And so He is, indeed.

> *And behold I am with you always, to the end of the age* (Matthew 28:20).

PHOTOGALLERY

Rome, 2008 Dignity of Women Conference with my good friends (from left to right) Donna Marie Cooper O'Boyle, Colleen Carroll Campbell, yours truly, Genevieve Kineke, and Elizabeth Kirk

Waiting for the private audience with the Holy Father in the Apostolic Palace; Dignity of Women Rome Conference, February, 2008.

At the EWTN studio to tape a feature on Colleen's show "Faith and Culture" with Colleen Carroll Campbell, Dale O'Leary, Donna Marie Cooper O'Boyle, Elizabeth Kirk, Genevieve Kineke, and myself

Thank you to EWTN for the use of these photos.

Doug Keck, executive producer of EWTN, interviewing yours truly, along with Janet Morana with the "Silent No More Awareness" campaign.

March for Life: Lisa Peters and Julie Hage from Pregnancy Aid in Detroit and Dave Palmer from Guadalupe Radio with me at the Family Research Council studios in D.C We did the show live from there.

Me and Janet Morana co-founder of Silent No More Awareness marching in the March for Life. Dr. Alveda King, the niece of the Rev Martin Luther King Jr. is next to Janet.

e, Dom, and Fr
ank Pavone National
r. Priests for Life at
e March for Life
se Dinner

The Voice of Women of Grace

40 July / August 2008 $7.95/$8.95 CAN

Donna-Marie Cooper O'Boyle
Women Thirsting for Living Water:
Mulieris Dignitatem and the International Women's Congress in Rome

Johnnette S. Benkovic
Our Lady of Mount Carmel, Her Scapular, Her School

Elena-Maria Vidal
Modest, not Frumpy: Beauty and the Blessed

20 YEARS   PLUS...

                    Patron Saint of Diabetics ...
                    Catholic Abolitionists in the Dominican Republic ...
                    Encouragement for Stressed-Out Moms ...
                    Keeping Returning Soldiers Safe ...
                    ... and much more!

MULIERIS DIGNITATEM

I was honored to be on the cover of "Canticle" magazine with Cardinal Rylko,
head of Pontifical Council for the Laity and Donna Marie Cooper O'Boyle.

Dom and I joining our friend, EWTN Rome Bureau Chief, Joan Lewis, for dinner in the Eternal City, 2006.

My husband, Dom, and myself on a 2006 trip to Siena and Rome.

Dominic and I on
the Mount of Oliv
overlooking the O
City of Jerusalem,
2007.

Renewing our vows at the
Church of Cana in Galilee,
2007.

Site of the Dead Scrolls in Qumram, Israel, 2007.

Strolling through the Old City of Jerusalem, 2007.

(L to R) Janet Ray, Steve Ray, myself, and Dominic in our 2007 trip to the Holy Land.

Marissa Hornbuckle with Guadalupe Radio and Third Millennium Media at the Garden of Gethsemane April 2008

Steve and I along the Sea of Galille reporting live for Ave Maria/ EWTN radio.

Steve and I in Capernaum, the town of Jesus.

Joining pilgrims, and friendly camel, along the Palm Sunday route on the Mount of Olives.

To join us on a future pilgrimage visit my website www.TeresaTomeo.com or Steve's website www.CatholicConvert.com

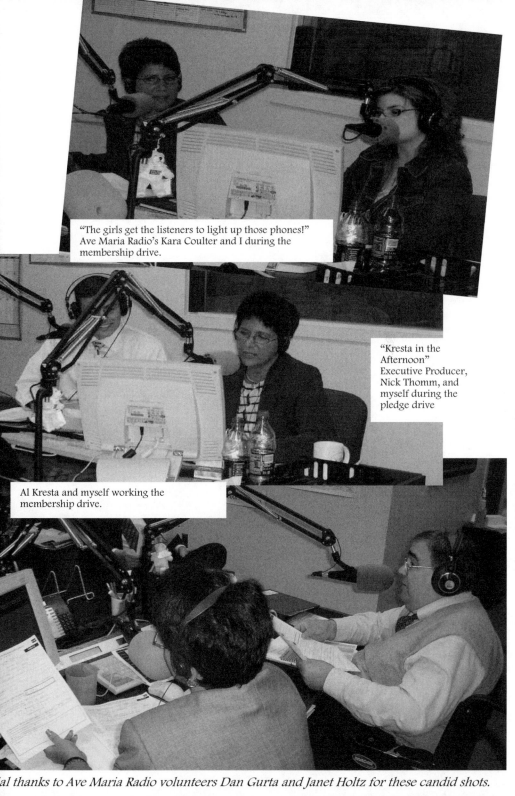

"The girls get the listeners to light up those phones!"
Ave Maria Radio's Kara Coulter and I during the
membership drive.

"Kresta in the
Afternoon"
Executive Producer,
Nick Thomm, and
myself during the
pledge drive

Al Kresta and myself working the
membership drive.

ial thanks to Ave Maria Radio volunteers Dan Gurta and Janet Holtz for these candid shots.

FOR THE READER

reflections
and
resources

My goal with this book is to give witness to the mighty works of God in my life. I want to give glory and honor to Him in all that I say and do. I also think of the many women I have met throughout my career who have fallen away from the Church. These women are in my heart as I write this book because I want to take their hand and walk them home to Rome. And, of course, I write this book so that all can be reminded of the graces and mercy of God. To that end I invite you now to reflect on the questions found in the following pages and use the space provided to record your thoughts and reactions, or simply allow yourself time in which to contemplate them. You might also consider buying a journal in which you can record yours answers, at length, for your own reflection.

I've also included a resource list that identifies, in one easy location, the different Scripture verses found throughout the book, the Catechism paragraphs referred to, and the papal documents from which excerpts were drawn.

Finally, I've provided a number of websites and organizations that I believe are valuable in our journeys as Christians.

NEWSFLASH: A NEWS BULLETIN OR BRIEF ITEM OF URGENT NEWS, OFTEN BROADCAST AT SHORT NOTICE INTERRUPTING A SCHEDULED PROGRAM.

- *In what way has the Lord provided you with "newsflashes" that were meant to get your attention?*
- *How did you respond to those "newsflashes?"*
- *How might your responses need to be changed?*

THE *"FIVE W'S AND THE H:"* IN JOURNALISM, ALSO SOMETIMES REFERRED TO AS *"THE SIX W'S"* ARE THE BUILDING BLOCKS FOR ANY GOOD NEWS STORY AND REFERENCE THE BASIC QUESTIONS JOURNALISTS ASK WHEN FIRST DOING THEIR HOMEWORK AND GATHERING FACTS; WHO, WHAT, WHERE, WHEN, WHY, AND HOW?

- *If you were to look at your life from a subjective point of view, how might you see the "who's," "what's," "where's," "when's", "why's," and "how's" of your life?*
- *Consider ways in which the Lord has used the "five w's and the h" to bring you to where you are today and how your journey has been enriched by them.*

_____

_____

_____

_____

_____

_____

_____

_____

_____

_____

_____

_____

_____

_____

_____

_____

_____

_____

_____

_____

EXTREME CLOSE-UP: A PHOTOGRAPHIC TERM USED TO DESCRIBE A TYPE OF CAMERA FRAMING OF A SCENE OR PERSON THAT PROVIDES A CLOSER VIEW THAN A CONVENTIONAL CLOSE-UP

- *The Lord, in His mercy, is always encouraging us to take a closer look at ourselves. Consider ways in which you have been given this opportunity and record some of the most difficult close-ups.*
- *Pray for ways in which you can use these close-ups for your own growth as a Christian.*

_____

_____

_____

_____

_____

_____

_____

_____

_____

_____

_____

_____

_____

_____

_____

_____

_____

_____

_____

_____

_____

_____

MASTER CONTROL: THE CENTER OF OPERATIONS FOR A RADIO STATION, TV STATION, OR A NETWORK, AND THE FINAL POINT BEFORE SIGNAL TRANSMISSION. IT IS STAFFED 24/7 TO ENSURE CONTINUOUS OPERATION.

- *Brainstorm a list of areas in your life that you have not yet given control to God.*
- *Select one or two areas that are the most challenging for you to let go and allow prayer time and conscious attention to be applied to them over the course of a few weeks or months and then re-evaluate those areas.*

_____

_____

_____

_____

_____

_____

_____

_____

_____

_____

_____

_____

_____

_____

_____

_____

_____

_____

_____

_____

_____

INTERRUPTED FEEDBACK: A COMMUNICATIONS SYSTEM USED IN TELEVISION WHERE THE ON-AIR FEED OR PROGRAM AUDIO BEING SENT TO THE REPORTER ON LOCATION IS INTERRUPTED WITH CUES OR DIRECTIONS FROM THE CONTROL ROOM. THE REPORTER WEARS A SMALL EARPIECE OR HEADSET COMMONLY REFERRED TO AS THE IFB.

- *Our natural inclination is often to listen to God but with interference we've generated on our own, or we completely remove ourselves from our ability to hear from Him. Consider ways in which you've interrupted His feedback and offer prayer time to re-establish that communication with Him. Record your experience.*

_____

_____

_____

_____

_____

_____

_____

_____

_____

_____

_____

_____

_____

_____

_____

_____

_____

_____

_____

PLEASE STAND BY: A PHRASE USED BY A TV OR RADIO ANNOUNCER TO INFORM THE AUDIENCE OF A TECHNICAL DIFFICULTY OR AN INTERRUPTION IN REGULARLY SCHEDULED PROGRAMMING .

- *Oftentimes the Lord is doing His very best to let us know that we ought to be "standing by" and listening to His message. He wants our program interrupted! In what way is God trying to interrupt your program but you may not be noticing? Record your thoughts.*

_____

_____

_____

_____

_____

_____

_____

_____

_____

_____

_____

_____

_____

_____

_____

_____

_____

_____

_____

_____

_____

_____

_____

SEGUE: A METHOD USED IN BROADCAST JOURNALISM TO SMOOTHLY TRANSITION FROM ONE SUBJECT MATTER TO THE NEXT SO AS NOT TO JAR THE LISTENER OR VIEWER.

- *Think about how you have handled change in your own life and what you might do differently?*
- *How can you make your own misery a ministry?*

_____

_____

_____

_____

_____

_____

_____

_____

_____

_____

_____

_____

_____

_____

_____

_____

_____

_____

_____

_____

_____

_____

ON ASSIGNMENT: A PHRASE APPLIED TO A JOURNALIST WHO IS GIVEN A SPECIFIC TOPIC OR ISSUE TO COVER OVER A LONG TERM BASIS.

- *What "assignments" do you believe you have been given?*
- *Eleanor Powell said "what we are is God's gift to us. What we become is our gift to God." How does this apply to your life right now?*

_____

_____

_____

_____

_____

_____

_____

_____

_____

_____

_____

_____

_____

_____

_____

_____

_____

_____

_____

_____

_____

_____

_____

_____

_____

SCOOP: AN INFORMAL NEWS REPORTING TERM USED TO DESCRIBE A MAJOR STORY OF GREAT SIGNIFICANCE, EXCITEMENT, AND ESPECIALLY SURPRISE- A STORY THAT REVEALS PREVIOUSLY UNKNOWN OR SECRETATIVE INFORMATION.

- *What did you learn about Catholic teaching in this chapter that you were not aware of before?*
- *What are some ways in which you will enrich your own knowledge about the faith?*
- *How can you help spread the word or the "scoop" about the Catholic faith?*

_____

_____

_____

_____

_____

_____

_____

_____

_____

_____

_____

_____

_____

_____

_____

_____

_____

_____

_____

_____

_____

_____

_____

DEVELOPING STORY: A STORY OF MAJOR SIGNIFICANCE UPDATED BY MEDIA OUTLETS ON A REGULAR BASIS WITH IMPORTANT INFORMATION OR "DEVELOPMENTS."

- *Are you happy with the way your life story is developing? What are ways in which it might still be improved as it develops?*
- *If not happy with the development of your own story, how do you think your Catholic faith can help you on the journey?*
- *Consider the sources your currently use or rely on. Do they stand up to your scrutiny? Are they reliable? Do you need new sources?*

_____

_____

_____

_____

_____

_____

_____

_____

_____

_____

_____

_____

_____

_____

_____

_____

_____

_____

_____

_____

_____

_____

1. Papal documents referred to throughout the book can be found on the Vatican website at http://www.vatican.va/. Specifically, we used excerpts from the following documents:

    a. John Paul II; Mulieris Dignitatem; 1988

    b. John Paul II address to members of the International Catholic Union of the Press; December 6, 2002

    c. John Paul II; Laborem exercens; 1981

    d. Pope Leo XIII; Exeunte Iam Anno; 1888

    e. Pope Pius XII; Mediator Dei; 1947

    f. Pope Leo XIII; Arcanum; 1880

    g. Pope Pius XI; Casti Connubii; 1930

    h. Pope Paul VI; Humanae Vitae; 1968

    i. John Paul II; 1995 Letter to Women

    j. His Holiness Benedict XVI; address to gathering at National Shrine of the Immaculate Conception, Washington D.C; April 16th, 2008

2. The Catechism of the Catholic Church was used to support some of my thoughts as well as to inspire the reader to understand, more thoroughly, the teachings of the Church (see copyright page). Specifically, we cited lines from the following Catechism paragraphs in this book:

    a. 2283

    b. 526

    c. 2424

    d. 1779

    e. 2207

    f. 164

    g. 165

    h. 1696

    i. 1889

    j. 2270-74

    k. 2370

    l. 1785

3. The New American Bible, Saint Joseph Edition, was used for our Scripture quotes (see copyright page). Specifically we referred to the following verses:

  a. Revelation 4:11
  b. John 14:32; 3:20; 16:13a; 15:5
  c. Romans 8:22, 28; 10:17
  d. Galatians 6:6-10
  e. 1 Corinthians 2:9
  f. Matthew 16:24-26; 11:25-30; 9:37
  g. Hebrews 13:8
  h. James 4:2-3
  i. Psalm 46:10; 27:14
  j. Hosea 2:14
  k. 1st Peter 2:9; 3:15; 4:19
  l. Isaiah 30:15; 5:8; 61:3
  m. Luke 1:49
  n. Ephesians 3:20-21

4. Other books or publications I've referred to within this book include:

  a. Father Hardon's "Modern Catholic Dictionary," Eternal Life Publishing
  b. "Gates of Prayer: The New Union Prayerbook," Central Conference of American Rabbis, 1975

5. Websites I highly recommend, or have gathered information from, include:

  a. Marriage Encounter at www.me.org or www.marriage-encounter.org.
  b. American Psychological Association www.apa.org.
  c. Post Abortive Healing Resources:
      1. Silent No More Awareness Campaign; www.silentnomoreawareness.org
      2. Elliot Institute www.afterabortion.org .
      3. Priests for Life; www.priestsforlife.org
      4. Rachel's Vineyard www.RachelVineYardMinistry.org

5. Project Rachel www.hopeafterabortion.com

6. Abortion Breast Cancer Coalition www.abortionbreastcancer.com

d. Media Resources

    1. www.TeresaTomeo.com

    2. www.CatholicExchange.com

    3. www.vatican.va

    4. www.BezalelBooks.com

    5. Parents TV Council www.parentstv.org

    6. Media research center www.mediaresearch.org

    7. Culture and Media Institute www.CultureandMediaInstitute.org

    8. Catholic World News www.cwnews.com

ABOUT THE AUTHOR

Teresa Tomeo is an author, syndicated Catholic talk show host, and motivational speaker with nearly 27 years of experience in communications as a talk show host, radio and TV news woman, and newspaper columnist.

Teresa left the secular media in 2000 to start her own speaking and communications company. Teresa's daily morning program, **"Catholic Connection"**, is produced by Ave Maria Radio in Ann Arbor, Michigan and heard on over 120 Catholic stations through EWTN Global Catholic Radio, as well Sirius Satellite Radio.

Teresa is a columnist and special correspondent for the national Catholic newspaper, *"Our Sunday Visitor"*, as well as a writer for the *Zenit* Catholic News Agency. She has also appeared frequently on *EWTN Catholic Television* and has been featured on *"The O'Reilly Factor"* and *Fox News.*

Recently Teresa was chosen as only one of 250 women from around the world to serve as a delegate at the Pontifical Council for the Laity's International Women's Congress held in Rome, marking the 20th Anniversary of John Paul II's Letter *On the Dignity and Vocation of Women.*

As a speaker Teresa travels around the country addressing the topic of media awareness and activism, as well as sharing her faith journey and providing concerned citizens with the tools needed to stand up against the immoral aspects of today's culture. Her first book,*" Noise-How Our Media Saturated Culture Dominates Lives and Dismantles Families",* was published by Ascension Press. *"Noise"* is a Catholic best-seller and is now in its second printing. Her second book, *" Newsflash! My Surprising Journey from Secular Anchor to Media Evangelist"* is published by Bezalel Books.

Teresa's website is **www.TeresaTomeo.com.**

*God withholds Himself
from no one who
perseveres.*

Teresa of Avila